Languages of the
World/Materials

501

ከወደ፡ ንዕራሉ ሱር፡ ግሮ ሱር፡ ሕ ጸረ፡
ዛሩሁቁ፡ ኢ ፉ ሸ ሪ፡ ዖር፡፡

ለ ፉ ጸ ? 9.6.207

ኢን ሱ ሱ ፡ ተ ፉ ሁ

full text research
abstracts of all titles
monthly updates

LINCOM webshop
www.lincom-europa.com

Sidaama (Sidaamu Afoo)

Anbessa Teferra

2014
LINCOM GmbH

Published by LINCOM GmbH 2014.

LINCOM GmbH
Hansjakobstr.127a
D-81825 Muenchen

LINCOM.EUROPA@t-online.de
www.lincom.eu

webshop: www.lincom-shop.eu

Bibliographic information published by the Deutsche Nationalbibliothek

The Deutsche Nationalbibliothek lists this publication in the Deutsche Nationalbibliografie; detailed bibliographic data are available in the Internet at http://dnb.dnb.de

Printed in E.C.
Printed on chlorine-free paper

ACKNOWLEDGEMENTS

I am indebted to several people whose support was crucial for the undertaking of this research. First of all, I want to express my heartfelt thanks to Prof. Shlomo Izre'el, my department chairperson and colleague. It was upon his suggestion that I decided to write this grammatical sketch of Sidaama. Later on, he commented on individual chapters of the book and suggested various revisions and additions.

I want to thank Prof. Grover Hudson for his incisive comments and corrections throughout the book. Had it not been for his constant advice, the book would not have attained its present form. I was specially touched by his prompt replies for all my correspondences. He also sent me various materials on Cushitic languages.

Let me express my gratitude to Dr. Azeb Amha for providing me with various research papers and books which were essential for my research. I wish also to thank Aadde Waayyiso who was the program manager of Sidaama Radio for sending me necessary materials on the language and for his advice regarding some cultural practices of the Sidaama.

I also thank my cousin *Kalaa* Seifu Taddese and my younger brother *Kalaa* Melkamu Teferra who sent me the "*Woganke*" and "*Fichchee*" magazines (which are published during the annual Sidaama Language and Culture Symposium) and other relevant books on the language.

I would also like to thank Girum Tesfaye for e-mailing me a PDF of his M.A. thesis entitled "*Ideophones in Sidaama: Documentation and Description*".

Last but not least, I would like to thank my spouse Woizero Aregash Haile Mariam who stood by my side and always encouraged me during the course of this research.

To Rachel, Yared, and Hanoch

TABLE OF CONTENTS

6

8

List of Tables

Abbreviations and Symbols

→	it becomes	INTR	intransitive
-	morpheme boundary	JUSS	jussive
.	(a) separates metalanguage elements	LOC	locative
/ /	underlying/phonological form	M	masculine
[ ]	phonetic form	NEG	negative
*	ungrammatical or hypothetical form	NMZ	nominalizer
?	unclear grammatical status	NOM	nominative (case)
ABL	ablative	NP	noun phrase
ABS	absolutive/citation form (case)	PASS	passive
ADV	adverbial phrase	PERF	perfective
AGT	agentive	PL	plural
AP	adjectival phrase	POL	polite
CAUS	causative	POST	postposition
CONT	continuous aspect marker	PP	postpositional phrase
COP	copulative verb	PPERF	present perfect
CNV	converb	PRES	present
DAT	dative	PRVN	preventive
DBL	double causative	Q	question marker
EE	epenthetic element	REFL	reflexive

EMPH	emphatic	REL	relative marker
F	feminine	SG	singular
GEN	genitive case	SGV	singulative
IMP	imperative	TR	transitive
IMPERF	imperfective	VP	verb phrase
IMPRS	impersonal	1	1st person
INST	instrumental	2	2nd person
INT	intensive	3	3rd person

1. Introduction

This book deals with the grammar of Sidaama and is divided into five chapters. The first chapter is the introduction. It provides background information about the Sidaama language and its speakers, relevant sociolinguistic data, and review of the previous grammatical studies on the language. The second chapter deals with segmental phonemes and various phonological processes of the language involved in inflection and derivation. The third chapter deals with lexical and morphological categories and it covers various word classes, inflection, derivation, and compounding. The fourth chapter deals with phrasal categories. The phrasal portion involves the identification and analysis of major phrasal categories such as noun phrase, verb phrase, adjectival phrase, etc. The fifth chapter concerns syntax. In this section basic sentence types such as declarative, interrogative, negative, and imperative plus their subtypes are analyzed. Moreover, complex sentences which arise via sentential subordination or coordination are discussed. The final chapter contains two texts with morpheme-by morpheme inter-linear translation and free translation.

1.1 Classification of the Sidaama Language

Sidaama is a Highland East Cushitic (HEC) language. The HEC group comprises in addition to Sidaama languages such as Hadiyya, Kambaata, Alaba, Qabeena, Gedeo, and Burji. HEC is a member of the Cushitic family which is itself a member of the Afro-Asiatic phylum. The self-name of Sidaama is /**Sidaam-u afoo**/ (lit. 'Sidaama-of mouth) 'the Sidaama language'.[1]

Although Sidaama is spoken in a larger area than other HEC languages, it does not exhibit substantial dialect differences among speakers of different areas. According to the author, there are two varieties of Sidaama: the ʔaliččo ("highland") dialect and the **gammojje** ("lowland") dialect. The difference between these two dialects is minimal and involves a few phonological and lexical differences. For instance, in the ʔaliččo dialect there is a tendency to use /ɗ/ whereas the **gammojje** dialect prefers /t'/ as in. ɗagge vs. t'agge 'legend', ɗank'o vs. t'ank'o 'double pronged', ɗeerto vs. t'eerto 'far away', etc. Following are examples of lexical differences.

---

[1] The Sidaama language was previously known in the literature as *Sidamo*. However, the name *Sidaama* was adopted for two reasons. First of all the speakers of the language refer to their language and their ethnic group as *Sidaama*. For instance when asked about their identity they say: **ninke Sidaama-ho**. **k'al-i-nke Sidaama-ho** 'We are Sidaama. Our language is Sidaama' (*lit.* 'we-Sidaama-COP. word-NOM-our COP Sidaama-COP'). It is on basis of this fact that the Sidaama Language Committee adopted this name (Yohannes Latamo, personal communication). In addition, up to 1992, the term Sidamo was misleading because it was also the name of the province where Sidaama and also other languages were spoken.

ʔaliččo	Gammoojje	
hojja	č'alla	'alone'
koša	guda	'finish'
bak'ata	t'ook'a	'flee'

1.2 Geographical and Cultural Information

Sidaama is spoken in the Sidaama administrative zone of south-central Ethiopia, one of nine found in the Southern Nations, Nationalities and People's State (SNNPR); see the attached Sidaama language map on page 13. It is spoken by a people calling themselves Sidaama. According to the 2007 national census of Ethiopia, the number of Sidaama mother tongue speakers is 2,925,171 (Central Statistical Authority 2010: 200). There are also other ethnic groups such as the Amhara, Wolayta, Kambaata, Hadiyya, Soddo, Silte, etc. who live interspersed among the Sidaama. Although most of the Sidaama live in their own zone, there are small enclaves of Sidaama populations among the neighboring Arsi Oromo, Guji Oromo, and Gede'o.

The Sidaama zone is divided into 19 districts. Except for Omotic speaking Wolaytas in the west, the Sidaama are bounded by speakers of Cushitic languages. Guji Oromo in the east, Arsi Oromo in the north, and Gede'o speakers in the south. Sidaama is an ever-green area with varied topographical features including mountains, valleys, and plains, and fed by big rivers including the Gidaawo, Loggita, Gannale. Awasa, the smallest lake of the Great Rift Valley, is located in this zone. Topographically Sidaama comprises three altitudinal zones: the highlands **ʔaliččo**, midlands and lowlands **gammoojje**.

Most of the Sidaama are subsistence farmers, while quite few of them are pastoralists. Several are engaged in trade and government jobs. The types of crops cultivated are determined by the altitude. In the highlands they cultivate Ensete ventricosum the so-called 'false banana', barley, wheat, and, bamboo. The Sidaama represent an *ensete* culture, for whom the *ensete* plant form the main staple food which is supplemented occasionally by dairy products.

1.3 Status of the Language

Beginning from the 1950's Sidaama was used by Christian missionaries for preaching and also other religious practices. However, until the mid 1970's Sidaama was largely unused in public education. In the 1980's the military regime of Ethiopia permitted the use of fifteen languages in the on-going Mass Literacy Campaign, and Sidaama was one of those chosen languages.

During this period Sidaama and other languages were written using the Semitic Ethiopian script. However, because the codification was done inaccurately, reading and understanding the Sidaama primers was very difficult. This emanated from the difference in the number of

Figure 1.   Map of Sidaama Administrative Zone and its Districts (*wärädas*)

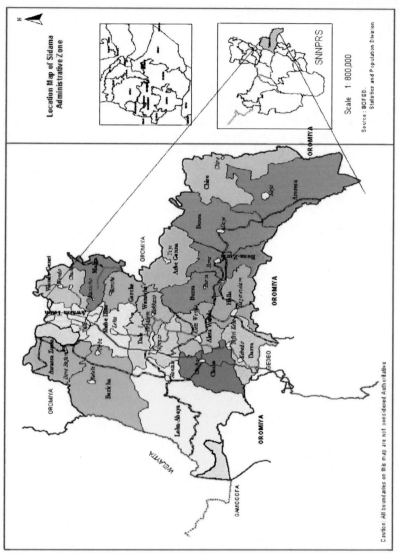

Source: **Sidaama Zone Finance and Economic Development Department (2011)**

14

vowels in Amharic and Sidaama, and inappropriate decisions regarding the representation of Sidaama vowels in the Ethiopic script. The selection of Sidaama as a language of literacy enabled the publication of several educational primers.

However, the most fundamental change with regard to the status of the Sidaama language took place in 1992. The then Transitional Government of Ethiopia (TGE) declared that each and every ethnic group can use its own language for primary education and also for official and administrative purposes.[2] Thus, since 1992, Sidaama is being used as a language of primary education and for administrative and judicial matters. In addition, permission was given to use any type of script to write the vernacular languages, and the Latin script was adopted for use in writing Sidaama. Since then a number achievements were recorded with regard to the linguistic development of Sidaama.[3] The main ones are: publication of teaching primers for elementary education, publication of books and magazines, audio recordings of songs, radio broadcasts, etc. Since September 2012 a program is opened at Hawaasa University to teach Sidaama linguistics at the B.A. level.

1.4 Review of Previous Studies

Major linguistic studies on Sidaama began during the Italian invasion of Ethiopia, towards the end of the 1930s. After a lull of twenty-five years a number of further publications were made on Sidaama, especially in the area of phonology, morphology and comparative linguistics. Some of the major works are briefly reviewed below.

Cerulli's **la Lingua e la Storia dei Sidamo** (1938) is a comparative grammatical and lexical work on Sidaama and related languages. Moreno's **Manuale di Sidamo** (1940) is a more cautious grammatical analysis owed to the fact that Moreno was one of the very few colonial Italian scholars of his time with a linguistic background. In **Manuale di Sidamo** Moreno deals with phonology, morphology and briefly with syntax. In addition his monograph contains texts and a host of exercises for the language learner, Sidamo-Italian and Italian-Sidamo glossaries, and, importantly, a section on "the position of Sidamo in Cushitic".

A. N. Tucker and M. A. Bryan (1966: 495-554) in their book **Linguistic Analyses. the Non-Bantu Languages of North-Eastern Africa** present Sidaama data which they excerpted from Moreno (1940) in side-by-side comparison with those of other Cushitic languages. Hudson

---

[2] Right of language usage is stated as follows in the Constitution of the Federal Democratic Republic of Ethiopia, in Article 39, No. 3. "Every Nation, Nationality and People in Ethiopia has the right to speak, to write and to develop its own language; to express, to develop and to promote its culture; and to preserve its history".

[3] The overall linguistic development of Sidaama, with a particular emphasis since 1993, will be treated in a separate research article.

(1976) is a comparative study of the five Highland East Cushitic languages. It includes phonology, morphology and a page or two of syntax. It is also the first formal comparative grammar on HEC languages. Still this work has very little material on the syntax of Sidaama.

Gasparini's **Grammatica practica della lingua Sidamo** (1978) is a monograph of word-class descriptions. It is largely limited to morphological description. The work also contains a wealth of illustrative data, various proverbs, puns, and a text entitled "Bokkili e Arfu".

Abebe *et.al* (1985) is a monograph which deals with the verb morphophonemics of five Highland East Cushitic languages. In the section devoted to Sidaama, Abebe deals with the canonical forms of the verb root, the various verbal inflections and derivations, and some major morphophonemic alternations. Wedekind's (1990) **Generating Narratives. Interrelations of Knowledge, Text variants, and Cushitic Focus Strategies** is the first discourse analysis ever done of the three HEC languages Gedeo, Burji and Sidaama. The main section of the book contains various narratives from the three languages and their discourse analysis. For instance the Sidaama section has two short texts.

Kazuhiro (2007) is a detailed grammar dealing with most aspects of the language from phonology up to semantics. Anbessa (2012) is a book version of his Ph.D. thesis. He treats phonology, morphology and syntax.

There are also a number of unpublished B.A and M.A theses written on linguistic aspects of Sidaama. For instance the author of this book himself wrote an M.A thesis entitled **Complement Clauses in Sidamo.**[4] In addition, a number of students who graduated from the Furra Institute of Development Studies in Yirgalem wrote their papers on Sidaama language and culture.[5]

Regarding dictionaries on Sidaama Gasparini's (1983) **Sidamo-English Dictionary** is a detailed one. It contains about 9000 lexical entries. His dictionary does not simply define a list of lexical items but also serves as a source of ethnological and cultural information regarding Sidaama society. With regard to Gasparini's dictionary Wedekind (*ibid.*, 25) writes, "It contains an unusually large amount of encyclopedic details about the Sidamo culture, and it is informative beyond the scope of a linguistic lexicon".

Hudson's (1989) **Highland East Cushitic Dictionary** is a comparative dictionary of five HEC languages. The author of this book served as one of the informants for the Sidaama data. In this dictionary Hudson compares words of the five HEC languages, Hadiyya, Kambaata,

---

[4] For a bibliography of Addis Ababa University theses on Sidaama, other langauages plus other sources refer to Hudson's web page at https://www.msu.edu/~hudson/HECrefs.htm.

[5] The Furra Institute of Development Studies was founded in 1997. It is one of the vital Sidaama teaching institutions for participatory integrated development studies.

Sidaama, Gedeo and Burji, side-by-side with Amharic and Oromo. After the comparisons, he presents wordlists of each HEC language with English translation. The final portion of his book is a list of Proto-HEC reconstructions.

There is also a **Sidama-Amharic-English Dictionary** of Indrias *et.al.* (2007). This dictionary in addition to the basic Sidaama lexemes, contains a wealth of newly created Sidaama words. It is meant not only for the general public but also to assist people working in offices and various governmental posts.

2. Phonology

In this chapter segmental phonemes, supra-segmentals, phonological and morphophonemic processes will be discussed.

2.1 Consonants

Sidaama has 24 consonant phonemes, displayed according to their place and manner of articulation in chart (1).

Table 1 Sidaama Consonant Phonemes

		Labial	Alveolar	Palatal	Velar	Glottal
Plosives	vl.	(p)	t	č	k	ʔ
	vd.	b	d	j	g	
Ejectives		p'	t'	č'	k'	
Implosive	vd.		ɗ			
Fricative	vl.	f	s	š		h
	vd.		(z)			
Nasals		m	n	ñ		
Liquids	lateral	l				
	flap	r				
Glides		w		y		

The phonemes /p/ and /z/ are placed in parenthesses because they are marginal phonemes. Both sounds are found only in loanwords used by educated speakers. Ex. **zufaane** 'throne' (Amh. **zufan**), **zoone** 'zone', **polise** 'police', **paarte** 'party', (all the three are are loans from English via Amharic), etc. The palatal stop /č/ has a very restricted distribution. Mostly it occurs as a geminate as in **guluččo** 'knee' or as a second member in a heterosyllabic sequence as in **danča** 'good'. The palatal nasal /ñ/ occurs only in a few verb stems some of which appear to be ideophones.

(1) a. **ñerri** **y-a**   b. **ñammi** **ʔass-a**
    nag   say-INF   taste   do-INF
    'to nag'   'to taste'

Consonants can occur both single and as geminates. Gemination is phonemic (contrastive) in Sidaama. All the consonant phonemes have a geminate counterpart as in some of the examples below.

(2) (a) i. **dana** 'appearance'   (b) i. **ʔada** 'paternal aunt'
      ii. **danna** 'forest'   ii. **ʔadda** 'truth'

(c)	i.	**gowa**	'to sew'	(d)	i.	**masa**	'to be startled'
	ii.	**gowwa**	'follish'		ii.	**massa**	'to take'
(e)	i.	**ka'a**	'to rise up'	(f)	i.	**guta**	'blade, main'
	ii.	**ka''a**	'to there'		ii.	**gutta**	'problem'

2.2 Consonant Allophones

The preglottalised flap [**'r**] is an intervocalic realization of /**ɗ**/. The following two examples illustrate its distribution where -a is the infinitive suffix.

(3) a./haɗ-a/ → [haʔr-a] 'to go'   b. /soɗ-a/ → [soʔr-a] 'to err'

However, the segment /ʔr/ can occur as part of a lexeme and not a phonetic realisation of /ɗ/ as in **goʔra** 'raspberry'.

Likewise [**w**] and [**h**] are intervocalic realizations of /**b**/ and /**k**/, respectively as shown below.

(4) c. /**gib-a**/ → [**giw-a**] 'to refuse'   d. /**gob-a**/ → [**gow-a**] 'to sew'
   e. /**duk-a**/ → [**duh-a**] 'to carry'   f. /**rak-a**/ → [**rah-a**] 'to be in a hurry'

2.3 Vowel Phonemes

There are five short oral vowels and five long counterparts.

		Front	Central	Back
High	short	**i**		**u**
	long	**ii**		**uu**
Mid	short	**e**		**o**
	long	**ee**		**oo**
Low	short		**a**	
	long		**aa**	

Vowel length is phonemic as in the following examples, where the suffix /**-a**/ marks the infinitive.

(5) a.	i	**kis-a**	'to touch'	b.	o	**dod-a**	'to run'
	ii	**kiis-a**	'to compensate'		oo	**dood-a**	'to dote'
c.	e	**deʔ-a**	'to forget'	d.	u	**fug-a**	'to suffocate'
	ee	**deeʔ-a**	'to defecate'		uu	**fuug-a**	'to swell'
e.	a	**mala**	'solution, plan'				
	aa	**maala**	'meat'				

The language has /ay/ diphtongs in words such as **haysso** 'grass' and **bayččo** 'place'. In addition, it has the nasal vowels **ā** and **ū** in ideophones such as **ʔāʔʔā y-a** 'to groan' and **hū ʔʔū y-a** 'to bellow'.

2.4 Syllable Structure

Syllable structure rules are a very important component of Sidaama phonology. Many of the phonological rules of the language arise from the need to preserve the syllable structure. The three main phonological processes in Sidaama and other HEC languages are **i**-epenthesis, nasal/glottal metathesis, and various assimilatory rules. These rules operate to satisfy syllable structure conditions. i.e., in order to ensure well-formedness of syllables.

Sidaama words begin with a consonant, and end in a vowel; within a word at most two consonants can occur between vowels, where Vy is counted as a diphthong. When syllables are considered, still the word-final syllable must be mentioned: vowel-final.

2.4.1 Overview of the Sidaama Syllable

Mono-syllabic simple words are very few, usually consisting of a consonant and long vowel.

(6) a. **t'a** 'now'   b. **lee** 'six'   c. **saa** 'cow'

A handful of the monosyllabics are verbs. Synchronically these verbs are mono-consonantal and become monosyllabic when verbal suffixes such as the infinitive suffix /-a/ are added.

(7) a. **š-a** 'to kill'   b.   **y-a** 'to say'[6]

Words range from bi-syllabic up to poly-syllabic. Every word in Sidaama must begin with a consonant as in **honse** 'nine' and must end in a vowel. As opposed to a word, a syllable can end either in a vowel as in **da.do** 'mat' or a consonant as in **lek.ka** 'foot'. In both examples and forthcoming ones the dot indicates a syllable boundary.

2.4.2 Canonical Syllable Forms

The language has both closed and open syllables. Closed syllables occur word internally in words such as **wol.k'a** 'power' and **dub.bo** 'forest'. However, open syllables tend to dominate since every word ends in a vowel. It is assumed that within a syllable an onset and nucleus are

---

[6] The verbs could be historically ***šiy-** 'kill' and ***yiy-** 'say'. This could provide a clue for the "sudden" lengthening of the vowel-initial nflectional suffixes. For instance /**-ummo**/ is '1MS.PERF'. If it is suffixed to the mono-consonatal verb stem /**y-**/ 'say', the output will be **yuummo** 'I said' (with mysterious lengthening of **u**) instead of the expected **yummo**.

obligatory while a coda is optional. This means a syllable can be open or closed. There are four canonical syllable types.

CV	**no**	'he is present'	**do.da**	'to run'
CVV	**maa**	'what?'	**see.da**	'tall/long'
CVC	**dib.be**	'drum'	**kin.čo**	'stone'
CVVC	**hayš.ša**	'to wash'	**baat.to**	'earth, land'

From the shape of the syllables it can be concluded that Sidaama has a light (CV), heavy (CVV)/ (CVC) and super heavy syllables (CVVC). As can be seen, all the syllables begin with a consonant, but they may end in a single vowel, a long vowel, or one consonant; but if the syllable is word-final, it must end in a vowel.

2.5 Consonant Sequences

Consonant sequences are heterosyllabic. There are three types of such sequences. sonorant-obstruent, sonorant-sonorant and glottal-sonorant ("glottalized continuants"). Below are given examples of each.

sonorant-obstruent

(i) a. **sir.ba** 'to sing'   b. **ʔan.ga** 'hand'   c. **wol.k'a** 'power'

sonorant-sonorant

(ii) a. **kor.ma** 'bull'   b. **gal.ma** 'a big house'   c. **šoy.loo** 'forty'

glottal-sonorant

(iii) a. **kaʔl-a** 'to help'   b. **maʔn.a** 'bed'   c. **goʔr.a** 'raspberry'

2.6 Stress

Stress is predictable, with exceptions, falling on the penultimate syllable of a word.

(8)   a. **míne** 'house'   b. **ʔáma** 'mother'

However, stress is final if the final vowel is long.

(9)   a. **mundée** 'blood'   b. **hunkée** 'sweat'

Exceptions are the 3rd. m. simple perfect, which contrasts with 2nd. singular jussive by stress, and the 3rd. m. present perfect, which contrasts with 1st plural jussive by stress.

(10) a. **dod-í** 'he ran'   b. **kubb-i-nó** 'he has jumped'
     dód-i 'run!'   **kúbb-i-no** 'let us jump'

2.7 Intonation Boundary

An intonation boundary is important in Sidaama. Depending on the point at which it is placed, the sentence can have different interpretations. Consider the example below where intonation boundary is indicated by a comma.

(11) a. **Samaago,   faraššo   guluf-í**
        Samaago   horse   ride-3MS.PERF
        'Samaago rode a horse.'

If the intonation boundary is placed in the above sentence after **faraššo** 'horse', then **Samaago** together with **faraššo** becomes a genitive construction forming together the object of the sentence. The subject is enclosed in parentheses to show its optionality.

b. **(ʔis-i),   Samaago   faraššo,   guluf-í**
     (he-NOM)   Samaago   horse   ride-3 M.SG.PERF
     'He rode Samaago's horse.'

2.8 Phonological Processes

As with other HEC languages, Sidaama observes a Two-Consonant Constraint whereby the maximum number of consonants in a sequence is two. All the morphophonemic processes arise from the need to preserve the above constraint and the syllable-structure rules. Morphophonemic processes are usually observed at the edge of verb stems, the place where stem-final consonants come into contact with consonant-initial inflectional suffixes. The main processes observed during such contacts are epenthesis, metathesis and various assimilatory processes.

2.8.1 Epenthesis

In verbal conjugations an epenthetic vowel is inserted under the following three conditions.
(i) When consonant-initial suffixes are added to mono-consonantal verb stems. The function of the epenthetic vowel /i/ is preventing a word-initial consonant sequence.

(12) a. /š-tú/   →   [šitú] 'She/They killed.'   /š-/ 'kill'
     b. /y-tú /   →   [yitú] 'She/They said.'   /y-/ 'say'

(ii) When consonant-initial suffixes are added to a verb stem which ends in a consonant sequence or geminate. In such cases epenthesis breaks a three consonant sequence.

(13) a. /sirb-tú /   →   [sirbitú] 'she/they sang'.   /sirb-/ 'sing'
     b. /kubb-tú /   →   [kubbitú] 'she/they jumped'.   /kubb-/ 'jump'

(iii) When a single causative /-s/ or a double causative /-siis/ suffix is added to a stem-final single obstruent.

(14) a. /ʔit-s-a/ → [ʔitis-a] 'to feed'
    b. /ʔit-siis-a/ → [ʔitisiis-a] 'to cause to be eaten'

2.8.2 Metathesis

There are two types of metathesis: nasal metathesis and glottal metathesis.

(i) Nasal Metathesis

This is a widespread process. The suffix-initial /-n/ is permuted with a stem-final single obstruent. The exception is a stem-final glottal stop in words such as /laʔ-/ 'see', /saʔ-/ 'pass', etc. which doesn't necessitate metathesis. Metathesis is necessitated in order to yield the preferred sonority structure of consonant sequences. Sidaama disallows the sequence of an obstruent and sonorant consonant but allows sonorant-obstruent sequences, and nasal metathesis results in exactly the latter type of sequence. The examples in (15) are based on /-nummo/, the 1st-person plural perfect suffix.

	verb stem				
(15)	/gib-/		'refuse'	/ginbummo/	'we refused'
	/ʔit-/		'eat'	/ʔintummo]/	'we ate'
	/hajaj-/		'order'	/hajanjummo/	'we ordered'
	/duk-/	+/-nummo/	'carry' →	/dunkummo/	'we carried'
	/bic'-/		'scratch'	/binc'ummo/	'we scratched'
	/ʔaf-/		'know'	/ʔanfummo/	'we knew'
	/kis-/		'touch'	/kinsummo/	'we touched'

(ii) Glottal Metathesis

Glottal metathesis is a process whereby the reflexive suffix /-ɗ/ is transposed with stem-final single sonorant consonant. The reflexive suffix i.e. /-ɗ/ changes to /ʔ/ when it comes into contact with a sonorant. Then it metathesizes with stem-final single sonorant. The examples below are based on the reflexive /-ɗ/ which is followed by the infinitive /-a/.

(16) a. /tum-/ 'pound'   [tuʔma] 'to pound for oneself'
    b. /fan-/ 'open' + /-ɗ-a/   [faʔna] 'to open for oneself'
    c. /kul-/ 'tell'   [kuʔla] 'to tell for one's benefit'

The exception to this rule is a stem-final /r/ which undergoes total assimilation instead of metatehsis as shown below.

(17) d.　/dar--/　'split' + /-ɗ-a/　　[daɗɗa]'to split for oneself'

In addition, a stem-final glottalized sonorant as in /gaʔm-/ 'bite' is considered as a sequence of two consonats and hence resists metathesis. Instead the usual rule of epenthesis applies to break the sequence of three consonants. In such a process /-ɗ/ becomes [-ʔr] because it occurs intervocalically.

(18) f.　/gaʔm-/　'bite' + /-ɗ-a/　　[gaʔmiʔra]　'to bite oneself'

2.8.3 Assimilation

Assimilation can be either partial or total and it takes place in order to assure the correct syllable-structures. Below we shall discuss each type of assimilation.

2.8.3.1 Partial Assimilation

The only example of partial assimilation is a homorganic nasal assimilation. This process causes a nasal to copy the place-of-articulation feature of a following obstruent. In most cases homorganic nasal assimilation takes place after nasal metathesis. The formatives involved in the data are /-nummo/ '1ˢᵗ PL.PERF' and /-tú/ '3 F.SG.PERF//3ʳᵈ PL.PERF'.

(19)　/gib-/　　　　　　　'refuse'　[gimbummo]　'we refused'
　　　/ʔaf-/　　　　　　　'know'　　[ʔaɱfummo]　'we knew'
　　　/hajaj-/　+/-nummo/　'order' →　[hajañjummo]　'we ordered'
　　　/duk-/　　　　　　　'carry'　　[duŋkummo]　'we carried'
　　　/morom-/ +/-tú/　　'deny'　　[morontú]　　'she/they denied'

2.8.3.2 Total Assimilation

Sidaama does not allow adjacent consonants with like sonority to differ in other features. When suffixation leads to such ill-formed clusters total assimilation takes place to resolve it. The assimilation is progressive. that is, the latter consonant assimilates to the former. Two types of total assimilation are observed: obstruent assimilation and sonorant assimilation.

(i) Progressive Total Obstruent Assimilation

This type of assimilation occurs when a suffix with initial /t/ is attached to stem-final obstruents. The examples below are based on /-tú/, the '3 F.SG.PERF//3ʳᵈ PL.PERF'suffix.

(20)　a.　/gib-/　　'refuse'　[gibbú]　'she/they refused'
　　　b.　/led-/　　'add'　　[leddú]　'she/they added'
　　　c.　/bat'-/　'like'　　[batt'ú]　'she/they liked'

24

d. /hajaj-/   'order'   [hajajjú] 'she/they ordered'
e. /duk-/ +/-tú/   'carry'   [dukkú] 'she/they carried'
f. /laʔ-/   'see'   [laʔʔú] 'she/they saw'
g. /ʔaf-/   'know'   [ʔaffú] 'she/they knew'
h. /mis-/   'become fat'   [missú] 'she/they became fat'

(ii) Progressive Total Sonorant Assimilation

Suffix-initial /n/ is totally assimilated to a stem-final single sonorant consonant.

	/-nummo/	'1st PL.PERF'	[kullummo]	'we told'
(21) /kul-/ 'tell' +	/-nó/	'3rd M.SG.PERF	[kulló]	'he has told'
	/-nò/	'1st PL.JUSS'	[kullò]	'let us tell!'
	/-ní/	'3rd POL.PERF'	[kullí]	'he (pol.) told'

(iii) Regressive Total Obstruent Assimilation

Regressive total obstruent assimilation takes in the intensive stem whereby a monosyllabic stem is repeated with a total assimilation of the middle consonants.

(22) a. /kub-/ 'jump' /kubkub-/ → [kukkub-] 'jump repeatedly'
     b. /k'as-/ 'stab' /k'ask'as-/ → [k'akk'as-] 'stab repeatedly'
     c. /kad-/ 'kick' /kadkad-/ → [kakkad-] 'kick repeatedly'

(iv) Ejectivization

Ejectivization is another type of assimilation and it takes place upon suffixation of the reflexive morpheme /-ɗ/ after a stem-final single obstruent and /r/. The obstruents become long ejectives, and /r/ becomes ɗɗ.

(23) a. /dib-/   'cover' /dipp'-/   'cover oneself'
     b. /sut-/   'hang'   /sutt'-/   'hang for oneself'
     c. /hajaj-/ 'order' +/-ɗ/ → /hajačč'-/ 'order for oneself'
     d. /daak-/ 'grind' /daakk'-/ 'grind for oneself'
     e. /wor-/   'put'   /woɗɗ-/   'put for oneself'

2.8.4 Weakening (Lenition)

The stops /b/, /ɗ/ and /k/ change to /w/, /ʔr/ and /h/, respectively in intervocalic position. The lenition examples are based on /-i/, the 3rd M.SG.PERF suffix.

(24) a. /duub-/ 'be satisfied' [duuwí] 'he was satisfied'

b. /haɗ-/   'go'   +/- í/   [haʔrí]   'he went'

c. /duk-/   'carry'   [duhí]   'he carried'

2.8.5 Vowel Elision

Vowel elision takes place in fast speech when /di-/, the negative morpheme, is prefixed to ʔ-initial verb stems. In such conjugations the final vowel of /di-/ i.e. /i/ and the initial /ʔ/ of the verb stems are deleted. The examples are based on /-oommo/, the 1st M.SG.PPERF present perfect suffix.

	Underlying Form		Deletion of i and ʔ		
(25) a.	/di-ʔagoommo/	→	[dagoommo]	'I have not drunk'	/ʔag-/ 'drink'
b.	/di-ʔoloommo/	→	[doloommo]	'I haven't thrown'	/ʔol-/ 'throw'
c.	/di-ʔumoommo/	→	[dumoommo]	'I haven't dug'	/ʔum-/ 'dig'

2.8.6 Elision of /h/

In fast speech, stem-initial /h/ is deleted between vowels. This takes place when the negative prefix /di-/ precedes verb stem-initial /h/. The elision of /h/ consequently will lead to a sequence of two dissimilar vowels and one of them may be elided as above. The examples show /-anno/, the 3rd M.SG.IMPERF suffix.

	Underlying Form		Deletion of h		Deletion of i	
(26)	/di-has-anno/	→	/di-as-anno/	→	[dasanno]	'he will not look for'
	/di-hab-anno/	→	/di-ab-anno/	→	[dawanno]	'he will not forget'
	/di-hankʼ-anno/	→	/di-ankʼ-anno/	→	[dankʼanno]	'he will not become angry'

2.9 Morphophonemic Processes

These are grammatically conditioned processes. The only example of a morphophonemic process in Sidaama is total gemination in 2 PL.IMP forms. In such forms any type of stem-final single consonant is geminated. Consider the data in (27).

(27)	/gib-/	'refuse'	[gibbe]	'refuse (pl.)!'
	/led-/	'add'	[ledde]	'add (pl.)!'
	/hajaj-/	'order'	[hajajje]	'order (pl.)!'
	/laʔ-/	'see'	[laʔʔe]	'see (pl.)!'
	/kis-/	'touch'	[kisse]	'touch (pl.)!'
	/morom-/	'deny'	[moromme]	'deny (pl.)!'
	/fan-/	'open'	[fanne]	'open (pl.)!'
	/kul-/	'tell'	[kulle]	'tell (pl.)!'

3. Morphology

Sidaama has major and minor lexical categories. The major ones include content words such as nouns, pronouns, adjectives, and adverbs. These four lexical categories are major in the sense that they can occur as heads of constituents. The minor lexical category subsumes postpositions and specifiers which can be labeled as function words.

3.1 Nouns

A noun in its citation form consists of a noun stem, an optional singulative marker (-(č)čo), and a terminal vowel. A noun stem is always consonant-final. The terminal vowel of a noun in its citation form can be one of three vowels: /e/, /a/, or /o/. In (28) below a sample list of both masculine and feminine nouns is provided with the terminal vowel indicated.

	Masculine		Feminine	
(28) a.	hayt'-e	'barley'	a. ʔill-e	'eye'
b.	ʔann-a	'father'	b. ʔam-a	'mother'
c.	hand-o	'ox'	c. ʔad-o	'milk'

Each one of the three terminal vowels can mark either masculine or feminine as is evident from the examples. Although no particular vowel is tied up with one of the genders, the vowel /e/ appears to be preponderant in feminine nouns. For instance loan nouns which end in consonants usually suffix /e/ to conform to a Sidaama constraint which bars words with a final consonant. The resultant noun is categorized as a feminine (irrespective of the size the loan word denotes) as the examples below show.

(29) a.	tank	tank-e	'tank'
b.	t'əyyət	t'iyyit-e	'bullet'
c.	awtobus	ʔotobus-e	'bus'

The typical categories for which nouns may be specified morphologically are number, gender, and case. Number and case features are quite regularly marked on nouns while gender is marked only on very few nouns.

3.1.1 Number

Count nouns by their very nature can co-occur with numerals as in. **sase minna** 'three houses'. Number is divided into three sub-types. singular, collective, and plural.

3.1.1.1 Singulative

In some nouns such as **hando** 'ox', **saa** 'cow', and **mine** 'house', the singular is morphologically unmarked.[7] In others singularity is indicated by a special formative known as *singulative*. According to Sim (1989. 105) singulative "...carries implications of particularity in discourse reference...". The singulative suffix is /-čo/ after stem-final sonorants and /-ččo/ elsewhere. Below are given a sample of singulative nouns.

(30) a. woš-i-ččo   b. dar-čo   c. badal-čo
     dog-EE-SGV   leaf-SGV   maize-SGV
     'dog'   'leaf'   'a maize cob'

     d. lukk-i-ččo   e. man-čo   f. mik'-i-ččo
       hen-EE-SGV   man-SGV   bone-SGV
       'hen'   'man'   'bone'

In some nouns which seem to have the singulative /-ččo/, the first /-č/ is not part of the singulative but is rather a result of regressive assimilation (spreading) of the singulative /-č/ to the stem-final consonant. The evidence for this comes from plural formation. When such nouns are inflected for plural, a stem-final consonant surfaces as shown below.

	Singulative		Plural		Noun Stem
(31) a.	ʔiwiiččo	'louse'	ʔiwiiw-e	'lice'	/ʔiwiib-/
b.	guluččo	'knee'	guluw-e	'knees'	/gulub-/
c.	daguččo	'cedar'	daguw-a	'cedar trees'	/dagub-/

In some other nouns which seem to have a singulative of the form /ššo/, the first /š/ is historical stem-final **s** or **d**, and the product of an earlier process by which the stem-final consonant /s/ or /d/ plus /-čo/ became /ššo/.

	Singulative		Plural	
(32) a.	hamaššo	'snake'	hamaso	< hamas-čo
b.	galaššo	'monkey'	galado	< galad-čo
c.	rumuššo	'root'	rumudda	< rumud-čo

Marking a single item is not the only grammatical role of singulative. It can also mark diminutiveness as in **beettiččo** 'a small girl'.

---

[7] A singulative of the form /–čč'o/ has the secondary function of marking diminutiveness in adjectives as the following examples illustrate.
   (a) **danč-i–čč'o** 'a beautiful little girl'.
   (b) **šiim–i–čč'o** 'a small one'
   (c) **faayy–i–čč'o** 'a pretty little one'

3.1.1.2 Collective

Some nouns have a collective form. In such nouns the collective is formed by suffixing either /-o/ or /-e/, to a noun stem.

	Singular	Collective	Plural	
(33) a.	faraššo	farad-o	farad-da	'horse'
b.	galaššo	galad-o	galad-da	'monkey'
c.	gereččo	gereew-o	gereeb-ba	'sheep'
d.	mančo	mann-a	mann-oota	'man'

Since a collective denotes a group of things as a single entity, it is inflected for singular and not plural.

(34) (a) mann-u,   sirb-í

      people-nom.   Sing-3SG.M.PERF

      'The people sang.'

   (b) *mann-u,   sirb-i-tú

      people-nom.   sing-EE-3PL.PERF

3.1.1.3 Plural

Compared to other HEC languages, Sidaama is rich in plural formation processes. There are at least seven different plural formation processes. The pluralization form for a given noun is not predictable. All the seven plural formation processes are exemplified below.

	Singular	Plural	
(35) a.	?awul-čo	?awull-a	'owl'
b.	?anna	?ann-uwa	'father'
c.	sikk'o	sikk'-ubba	'stick'[8]
d.	?agar-aančo	?agar-aasine	'guard'
e.	waajj-aančo	waajj-aano	'coward'
f.	gaango	gaang-oota	'mule'
g.	č'im-eessa	č'im-eeyye	'wiseman'

Irregular plural forms are very few. One of them is **meento** 'women' (its singular form is **mančo**) where /-t/ is perhaps the old Cushitic feminine marker. The plural of **beeto** 'boy' is **ooso** 'children' a good example of suppletion. According to Ferguson (Bender *et.al.*, 1976: 72) the co-occurrence of singular with numerals is an interesting aspect of Ethiopian

---

[8] There is also the variant **sikk'-uwa** 'sticks'.

languages. Thus, if a numeral precedes a singular noun, then the noun can optionally be in singular form. Although singular with numerals is possible, the preferred form in Sidaama is plural with numerals.

(36) **sase**　　**mat'aaffa**　　**hidɗ-ummo** (rather than **sase**　**mat'aafa** 'three book')
　　　three　　books　　　buy-1SG.M.PERF
　　　'I bought three books.'

Another characteristic of plurals is the feature which Hudson (1976. 252-3) terms 'polarity', the "reversal of gender between the singular and plural of nouns" and it characterizes almost all HEC languages. Polarity is clearly evident in demonstrative + noun structures such as in (37).

(37) a.　**kun-i**　　　　**beett-i**
　　　　this-NOM　　boy-NOM
　　　　'this (m.) boy'

　　b.　**tin-i**　　　　**seemmo**
　　　　this-NOM　　girl
　　　　'this (f.) girl'

　　c.　**kun-i**　　　　**seenn-i**
　　　　this (m.)-NOM　girls-NOM
　　　　'these girls'

3.1.2 Gender

Sidaama is not rich in gender marking. Nevertheless there are a handful of distinctions and these are marked either lexically or by means of gender-marking suffixes.

(i)　Some kinship terms and common domestic animals distinguish gender lexically.

	Masculine		Feminine	
(38) a.	**hando**	'ox'	**saa**	'cow'
b.	**booto**	'bull'	**wo'riččo**	'heifer'
c.	**wosiila**	'maternal uncle'	**laʔlama**	'maternal aunt'

(ii) In very few nouns gender distinction is expressed by gender-marking suffixes: /**-tičča/** ~ /**-eessa/** marks masculine and **-titte**/ ~ /**-eette/** marks feminine. The basis of choice between the members of these pairs is morphological. For instance nouns ending in /**-tičča/** take masculine verb agreement while those ending in /**-eessa/** take femimine verb agreements.

	Masculine	Feminine
(39) a.	**moo-tičča**[9]	**moo-titte**
	'ruler/master'	'ruler/mistress'
b.	**soor-eessa**	**soor-eette**
	'first/leader' (M)	'first/leader' (F)

(iii) In two of the kinship nouns, feminine is marked by /-ee ~ -e/ while the masculine is unmarked.

	Masculine		Feminine	
(40) a.	**ʔahaaho**	'grandfather'	**ʔahaah-e**	'grandmother'
b.	**ʔaroo**	'husband'	**ʔar-ee**	'wife'

Inanimate nouns do not mark gender lexically and hence in such nouns gender is arbitrary. For instance, **k'amade** 'wheat' is feminine while **hayt'e** 'barley' is masculine. The gender of inanimate nouns is apparent in the morphological features which the particular noun selects. These include case, number, types of demonstratives which precede it, and agreement features with the verb. Nevertheless body parts appear to be feminine conforming to the general Afroasiatic tendency. The following words exemplify this fact.

(41) a.	**ille**	'eye'	c.	**lekka**	'foot/leg'
b.	**mačč'a**	'ear'	d.	**ʔanga**	'hand'

Some nouns are epicene, i.e. in their citation forms they refer to either sex. These include **beetto** 'boy'/'girl', **mančo** 'man'/'woman' and **rodoo** 'brother'/'sister'. Hence such nouns have dual meanings when they occur in their citation forms, for instance as verb objects. The exact gender of epicene nouns is revealed when they occur in subject position, where gender of the noun can be inferred from the nominative case-marking: masculine nouns are marked for nominative while feminine nouns are unmarked. Consider the two examples below.

(42) a.	**seed-u**	**beett-i**	**sirb-í**
	tall-NOM	boy-NOM	sing-3SG.M.PERF
	'The tall boy sang.'		
b.	**seeda**	**beetto**	**sirb-i-tú**
	tall	girl	sing-EE-3SG.F/3PL.PERF
	'The tall girl sang.'		

---

[9] Both the nouns **mootičča** and **mootitte** are derived from the verb stem **mook-** 'rule/reign' whereby the final **k** appears to be elided before the nominalizing suffixes.

In generic nouns the distinction between masculine and feminine is made by means of the gender qualifier **labbaa** 'male' and **mehaa** 'female' which are added before the respective nouns. Although the basic denotations of **labbaa** and **mehaa** are human male and female referents respectively, they can be extended to other animates. For instance **labbaa meʔiččo** is 'billy goat' while **mehaa meʔiččo** is 'she goat'.

3.1.3 Case

Case in Sidaama is divided in two classes: primary and postpositional. Primary cases are marked by a single vocalic suffix and comprise the nominative, absolutive, and genitive. Postpositional cases include the dative, instrumental, and ablative. These differ from the primary cases in that they are marked by the pospositions /-**nni**/ and /-**ra**/ suffixed to a genitive or an absolutive noun.

3.1.3.1 Nominative

Nominative is assigned to a subject NP of a finite or tensed clause. The nominative of masculine nouns is marked by /-**u**/ and /-**i**/. Feminine nouns are not marked overtly for nominative and hence remain in their citation forms.[10] The nominative allomorphs /-**u**/ and /-**i**/ are grammatically conditioned: /-**u**/ mostly marks a masculine nominative noun when this occur without modification (see (43), below), while /-**i**/ occurs elsewhere.[11] The examples in (43) exemplify a masculine and feminine noun in nominative function.

(43) a. **beet-u   lowo   ʔado   ʔag-í**
      boy-NOM   a lot   milk   drink-3SG.M.PERF
      'The boy drank a lot of milk.'

   b. **saa   hutt'a   hiikk'-i-tú**
      cow   fence   break-EE-3SG.F.PERF
      'The cow broke the fence.'

In noun phrases, a masculine nominative head is always marked by /-**i**/. Demonstratives precede the nominative head and they are always marked by /-**i**/. Regarding attributive adjectives there is a difference. Masculine adjectives are marked by /-**u**/ while feminine adjectives are unmarked as shown in (44).

---

[10] The only exception appears to be a relativized feminine form which is marked by /-**i**/ for nominative when it appears in subject position.
[11] The exception to this is the masculine noun **lemboola** 'pigeon', which takes /–**i**/ in the nominative. Even this is not fully an exception because **lemboola** has the singulative form **lemboolčo** which takes /–**u**/ as a nominative. **lemboolč–u** 'the pigeon'.

(44) a. **kun-i**   **beett-i**   **sirb-a**   **giw-anno**
this-NOM   boy-NOM sing-INF   hate-3SG.M.IMPERF
'This boy hates to sing.'

b. **seed-u**   **beett-i**   **min-i-ra**   **haʔr- í**
tall-NOM   boy-NOM home-EE-DAT go-3SG.M.PERF
'The tall boy went home.'

(ii) In genitives, a possessed masculine noun is marked by the nominative /-i/ while a possessed feminine is unmarked, as exemplified in (45).

(45) a. **dančile**   **ann-i**   **waa**   **ʔag- í**
Danchile   father-NOM water drink-3SG.M.PERF
'Danchile's father drank water.'

b. **dančile**   **ama**   **waa**   **ʔag-gú**
Danchile   mother water drink-3SG.F.PERF
'Danchile's mother drank water.'

(iii) Masculine proper nouns with final /a/ take /-i/ in nominative case. Masculine proper nouns which end in other vowels, i.e. /e/ and /o/ and all feminine proper nouns are unaffected. Consider the examples below in (46).

(46) a. **Samaago** **Yota** **kaʔl- í**
Samaago Yota help-3SG.M.PERF
'Samaago (M) helped Yota (M).'

b. **Yot-i**   **makina** **hiɗɗ-í**
Yota-NOM car buy-3SG.M.PERF
'Yota (M) bought a car.'

c. **Dančile** **ʔuddano** **hiɗɗ-i-tú**
Danchile cloth buy-EE-3SG.F.PERF
'Danchile (F) bought cloth.'

3.1.3.2 Absolutive

Absolutive is the lexical or citation form of a noun, as occurs also as an accusative, verb-object, noun. For instance **mine** is the lexical entry for 'house' and the accusative case form. That the citation or basic form is that of the accusative, and that the nominative is 'marked' by a suffix is rather unusual. Typically in languages of the world the accusative is marked. Marked nominative is, however, typical of languages of East Africa (König 2008). Absolutive (ABS) is not shown as a meaning in the morphological analysis of examples; it is evident by the absence of a nominative (NOM) suffix.

Consider the example below where **ʔado** 'milk' is in absolutive case since it is an object or accusative NP of the sentence.

(47) **beett-u,**   **ʔado**   **ʔag-í**
      boy-NOM   milk   drink-3SG.M.PERF
      'The boy drank milk.'

The absolutive can also function as a predicative nominal as in (48).

(48) (a) **kun-i**   **mine-ho**
         this-NOM   house-COP.M
         'This is a house.'

   (b) **kun-i**   **lowo**   **minee-ti**[12]
         this-NOM   big   house-COP
         'This is a big house.'

3.1.3.3 Genitive Case

If the genitive construction is possessor + possessed and a subject, then the genitive case of the possessor is marked /-**u**/ 'masculine (common noun)', /-**i**/ 'masculine (proper noun in final **a**)' and /-**te**/ 'feminine'.

(i) Masculine proper nouns which end in /a/ in their absolutive form take the genitive suffix /-**i**/, while those proper nouns ending in /-**e**/ or /-**o**/ remain unaffected.

	Proper Noun	Genitive Structure	
(49) a.	**daafursa** (m.)	**daafurs-i anna**	'Dafursa's father'
b.	**magane** (m.)	**magane anna**	'Magane's father'
c.	**leenjišo** (m.)	**leenjišo anna**	'Leenjisho's father'

(ii) If a genitive construction is possessor + possessed and a direct (verb) object, and the possessor is a common and not a proper noun, the genitive suffix is /-**u**/ for masculine possessor nouns and /-**te**/ for feminine possessor nouns. The possessed noun remains in its citation form.

---

[12] Note the lengthening of the final short vowel of **mine** before the neutral copula /-**ti**/. It appears this unique phonological process occurs only with this suffix.

34

(50) a. **manč-u**   **mine,**   **laʔ-ummo**
     man-GEN.M   horn   see-1SG.M.PERF
     'I saw the man's house.'

   b. **saa**-te   **faro,**   **laʔ-ummo**
     cow-GEN.F   tail   see-1SG.M.PERF
     'I saw the cow's's tail.'

When a genitive phrase occurs in subject position and the possessor is a common noun, the genitive suffixes of the possessor are /u/ and /te/ as above, while the nominative suffix /-i/ appears on masculine possessed nouns.

(51) a. **hand-u**   **buud-i,**   **kaajja-ho**
     ox-GEN.M   horn.M-NOM   strong-COP.M
     'The ox's horn is strong.'

   b. **saa-te₂**   **farr-i,**   **seeda-ho**
     cow-GEN.F   tail.M-NOM   long-COP.M
     'The cow's tail is long.'

A feminine possessed noun is unaffected (and appears in its citation form) because, as has been mentioned earlier, nominative is morphologically realized only on masculine nouns.

   c. **beetoo-te₂**   **ʔille,**   **hur-tú**
     girl-GEN.F   eye.F   heal-3SG.F.PERF
     'The girl's eye healed.'

Above we have seen genitive case marking in possessor + possessed structures. However, if the genitive construction involves only the possessor (as head noun), then with proper nouns and pronouns the genitive suffixes are /-h-u/ 'M', /-t-i/ 'F', and /-r-i/ 'PL' in nominative, and /-ha/ 'M', /-ta/ 'F' and /-re/ 'PL' in absolute. In the table below are provide genitive case declensions in nominative and absolute for pronoun, proper noun and common noun possessors.

Table 2. Genitive Case Marking in Possessor + Possessed Structures

(i) Pronoun Possessor (Nominative)		
(52) a. **ʔane-h-u**	b. **ʔane-t-i**	c. **ʔane-r-i**
1.SG-GEN.M-NOM	1.SG-GEN.F-NOM	1.SG-GEN.PL-NOM
'mine' (M)	'mine' (F)	'mine' (PL)
(ii) Pronoun Possessor (Absolutive)		
(53) a. **ʔane-ha**	b. **ʔane-ta**	c. **ʔane-re**

SG-GEN.M.ABS	1.SG-GEN.F.ABS	1. SG-GEN.PL.ABS
'mine' (M)	'mine' (F)	'mine' (PL)

(iii) Proper Noun Possessor (Nominative)

(54) a. **waayyiso-h-u**[13]	b. **waayyiso-t-i**	c. **waayyiso-r-i**
1.SG-GEN.M-NOM	1.SG-GEN.F-NOM	1.SG-GEN.PL-NOM
'Waayyiso's' (M)	'Waayyiso's' (F)	'Waayyiso's' (PL)

(iv) Proper Noun Possessor (Absolutive)

(55) a. **waayyiso-ha**	b. **waayyiso-ta**	c. **waayyiso-re**
1.SG-GEN.M.ABS	1.SG-GEN.F.ABS	1.SG-GEN.PL.ABS
'Waayyiso's' (M)	'Waayyiso's' (F)	'Waayyiso's' (PL)

(v) Common Noun Possessor (Nominative)

(56) a. **beetto-nni-h-u**	b. **beetto-nni-t-i**	c. **beetto-nni-r-i**
girl-PP-GEN.M-NOM	girl-PP-GEN.F-NOM	girl-PP-GEN-PL-NOM
'The girl's' (M)	'The girl's' (F)	'The girl's' (PL)

(vi) Common Noun Possessor (Absolutive)

(57) a. **beetto-nni-ha**	b. **beetto-nni-ta**	c. **beetto-nni-re**
girl-PP-GEN.M.ABS	girl-PP-GEN.F.ABS	girl-PP-GEN.PL.ABS
'The girl's' (M)	'The girl's' (F)	'The girl's' (PL)

When the possessor as head noun is a common noun, the postposition /-**nni**/ 'Instrumental/Ablative' (see below) must be suffixed to the noun as can be seen under (58) and (59).

3.1.3.4 Oblique Cases

Oblique case relations such as dative, instrumental, and ablative are marked by the postpositions /-**ra**/ and /-**nni**/ suffixed to an absolutive and a genitive base, respectively.

(i) Dative

The dative expresses the typically benefactive argument of a di-transitive verb and is marked by one of three postpositional morphemes suffixed to the absolutive. /-**ra**/ for pronouns and proper names, /-**ho**/ for other masculines, /-**te**/ for other feminines.

(58) a. **mančo**   **ʔate-ra**   **tima**   **ʔuy-tú-he**

---

[13] **Waayyiso** is a masculine proper noun.

woman   you-DAT   bread   give-3SG.F.PERF-you
'The woman gave you bread.'

b. **mančo**   **hando-ho**   **haysso**   **ʔuy-tú**
   woman   ox-DAT.M   grass   give-3SG.F.PERF
   'The woman gave grass to the ox.'

c. **mančo**   **saa-te**   **haysso**   **ʔuy-tú**
   woman   cow-DAT.F   grass   give-3SG.F.PERF
   'The woman gave grass to the cow.'

(ii) Instrumental and Ablative

Both the instrumental and ablative are expressed by /-**nni**/ which is suffixed to a genitive base.

(59) a. **harr-i-ččo**   **sikk'o-te-nni**   **gan-í**
       donkey-EE-SGV   stick-GEN.F-INST   beat-3SG.M.PERF
       'He beat the donkey with a stick.'

b. **man-č-u,**   **katam-u-nni**   **hig-í**
   man-SGV-NOM   city-GEN.M-ABL   return-3SG.M.PERF
   'The man returned from the city.'

3.1.4   Quantifiers

There are definite and indefinite quantifiers. Definite quantifiers comprise numerals and measure phrases. Numerals are cardinal and ordinal.

3.1.4.1 Cardinal Numerals

The cardinals for 1-10 are.

1	/mite/	6	/lee/
2	/lame/	7	/lamala/
3	/sase/	8	/sette/
4	/šoole/	9	/honse/
5	/ʔonte/	10	/tonne/

Cardinal numerals are used with count nouns.

(60) **sase**   **hand-a**   **hiɗɗ-ummo**

three ox-PL buy-1SG.M.PERF
'I bought three oxen.'

The numerals from 11 to 19 are pretty regular. They are formed from the numeral **tona** 'ten' (from **tonne** 'ten' with the ending /-a/) followed by the unit numerals. Thus **tona mite** 'eleven', **tona honse** 'nineteen'. The numerals from 20 to 90 are derived from the unit numerals but with vocalic and consonantal changes. The numerals 20, 30, and 40 have a final /-oo/ while numerals from 50 to 90 have final /-aa/.

20	/lemoo/	70	/lamalaa/
30	/sajjoo/	80	/settaa/
40	/šoyloo/	90	/honsaa/
50	/ʔontaa/	100	/t'ibbee/
60	/leyaa/	1000	/kume/

In order to combine unit numerals with the tens 20, 30, and 40 (in final **oo**) the suffix /-**iina**/ is added to the above numeral stems. Ex. **sajj-iina šoole** '34'. For the numerals 50 to 90 (in final **aa**) /-**yna**/ is added to the numeral stem as in **honsaa-yna sette** '98'.

3.1.4.2 Ordinal Numerals

Ordinal numeral formation is more complicated. These are formed first by suffixing the ordinal formative /-**kki**/. This base is followed by a genitive marker /-**h**/ 'masc.', /-**t**/ 'fem.' or /-**r**/ 'plural', and this is followed by a case marker /-**a**/ 'absolutive' or /-**u**/ 'nominative'.

The ordinal numerals second, third and sixth exhibit a sprouting of new sounds. Moreover, if an ordinal numeral stem ends in a sonorant consonant as in 2nd, 4th, 6th, and 7th, the first /k/ of the ordinal formative /-**kki**/ is elided.

1st	/mitt-i-kki-h-u/[14]	7^{Th}	/lamal-ki-h-u/
2nd	/layn-ki-h-u	8th	/sett-i-ki-h-u/
3rd	/say-kki-h-u/	9th	/hons-i-kki-h-u/
4th	/šool-ki-h-u	10th	/tonn-i-kki-h-u/
5th	/ʔont-i-kki-h-u/	11th	/tona mit-i-kki-h-u/
6th	/leel-ki-h-u/	22th	/lem-iina layn-kki-h-u/

3.1.4.3 Measure Phrases

---

[14] Also /ʔum–i–h–u/ 'the first' (lit. the head) or /ʔalb–i–h–u/ 'the first' (from /ʔalba/ 'face').

Numerals are used with count nouns only. Non-count nouns such as liquid, grain, flour, etc. on the other hand are specified by means of measure phrases. The measure phrases comprise a numeral and an obligatory head of the measure phrase which is connected with certain standards of measurement. The measure noun is almost always in singular. There are two types of measure nouns: traditional and modern. The former includes /**saffe**/ a grain measure, /**hoowo**/ 'palmful', /**č'igile**/ 'arms-length', etc. Modern measure nouns are exclusively loan words such as **kuntaala** 'sack', **t'armuse** 'bottle', **kiilo** 'kilogram', **farasula** 'a dry measure of 17 kilogram (usually for coffee beans)', etc. Two traditional measure nouns are presented in (61) and two modern measure nouns in (62).

(61) a. **sase   saffe   hayt'e**
　　　 three   vessel   barley
　　　 'three measures of barley'

　　b. **lame   č'igile   siiwo**
　　　 two   arm   rope
　　　 'two arms of rope'

(62) a. **mitto   kuntaala   bullee**
　　　 one   sack   flour
　　　 'one sack of flour'

　　b. **sasee   t'armuse   waa**
　　　 three   bottle   water
　　　 'three bottles of water'

3.1.4.4 Indefinite Quantifiers

Concrete nouns can be specified either by simple counting or by means of measure phrases. However, non-concrete (abstract) nouns such as **hagiirre** 'joy', **got'ano** 'sleep', **fooliiššo** 'rest' do not lend themselves to counting and measure phrases. Such nouns are quantified by words such as **šiima**, 'small/little', **manaado** 'average size', **lowo** 'big'.

Indefinite quantifiers may also occur with mass and count nouns.

(63) a. **lowo   waa**
　　　 big   water
　　　 'a large amount of water'

　　b. **šiima   buna**
　　　 small   coffee
　　　 'a small amount of coffee'

(64) a. **sase   minna**
　　　 three   houses
　　　 'three houses'

　　b. **lamala   sikk'ubba**
　　　 seven   sticks
　　　 'seven sticks'

3.1.5 Article

There is no morpheme to mark definiteness. Indefiniteness of human subjects can be indicated by using the numeral **mitt-e** 'one' (F), **mitto** 'one' (ABS.M) or **mitt-u** 'one' (NOM.M) as in **mitt-u man-č-i** 'a (certain) man' and **mitte mančo** 'a (certain) woman'.

3.1.6 Proper Nouns

Proper nouns may designate specific persons, places, or geographic features such as rivers, mountains, etc. as exemplified in (65).

(65) | Personal Names | River Names | Place Names |
|---|---|---|
| **Guyye** (m.) | **Gidaawo** | **Wondo** |
| **Dančile** (f.) | **Gambeeltu** | **Bansa** |
| **Daafursa** (m.) | **Waammoole** | **Yaanase** |

Unlike common nouns, proper nouns may be suffixed by the 'associative' suffix /-'o/ 'X and companions' as in **Beša-'o** 'Besha and her companions'.

3.2 Pronouns

There are personal, demonstrative, possessive, interrogative, relative, and reflexive pronouns in Sidaama.

3.2.1 Personal Pronouns

Personal pronouns distinguish nominative and absolutive case as in the table below. (The difference is not just different marks, but different forms.)

Table 3   Independent and Suffixed Nominative and Absolutive Pronouns

	Nominative		Absolutive		Absolutive Verb-Suffix	
Singular						
1ˢᵗ	**ʔan-i**	'I'	**ʔané**	me	**-ʔe**	me
2ⁿᵈ	**ʔat-i**	'you'	**ʔaté**	you.SG	**-he**	you.SG
3ʳᵈ M	**ʔis-i**	'he'	**ʔisó**	him	**-si**	him
3ʳᵈ F	**ʔise**	'she'	**ʔisé**	her	**-se**	her
Plural						
1ˢᵗ	**ninke**	'we'	**ninké**	us	**-nke**	us
2ⁿᵈ	**kiʔne**	'you'	**kiʔné**	you.PL	**-ʔne**	you.PL
3ʳᵈ	**ʔinsa**	'they'	**ʔinsá**	them	**-nsa**	them

Singulars of the independent nominative pronouns other than 3ʳᵈ F are marked by nominative **-i**. The 2ⁿᵈ PL. and 3ʳᵈ PL are used to express the 2ⁿᵈ and 3ʳᵈ polite, respectively. The pronoun paradigms do not make a masculine and feminine distinction in 1st and 2nd persons, as will be seen below in verb paradigms.

With verb-subject agreement expressed by verb-suffixes, independent pronoun subjects are usually redundant and hence omitted in sentences. However, absloutive independent pronouns are obligatory in cleft sentences as illustrated below.

(66) **ʔado   ʔag-ootto-h-u**   **ʔaté-ti**
     milk   drink-2M.SG.PPERF-REL.M-NOM   2.SG.Acc-COP.F
     `It is you who has drunk the milk.'

There are two types of absolutive pronouns: independent and suffixed. The absolutive independent pronouns are marked by a stressed final vowel.[15] The suffix absolutive pronouns express the object of verbs.

(67)   **kaaʔl-í-ʔe**
        help-3SG.M.PERF-**me**
        'He helped **me**.'

3.2.2 Demonstrative Pronouns

Demonstrative pronouns have three grades: *proximal* (*near*), *distal* (*far*), and *remote* (*very far*), expressing location relative to the speaker.

(68) a. **kuni** 'this (M)'   b. **kuuʔu** 'that (M)' (far)   c. **kuʔʔu** 'that (M)' (very far)

Demonstratives are marked for case, number and gender. All the various types of demonstratives are displayed in Table 4.

Table 4   Nominative and Absolutive Demonstrative Pronouns

		Nominative		**Absolutive**
'this'	M	**kun-i**	M	**konne**
'this'	F	**tin-i**	F	**tenne**
'these'	PL	**kur-i**	PL	**kore**
'that' (far)	M	**kuuʔ-u**	M	**kooʔe**
'that' (far)	F	**tiiʔ-i**	F	**teeʔe**
'that' (remote)	M	**kuʔʔ-u**	M	**koʔʔee**
'that' (remote)	F	**tiʔʔ-i**	F	**teʔʔee**
'those' (remote)	PL	**kuʔʔur-i**	PL	**koʔʔore**

---

[15]   Hudson (ibid., 257) failed to indicate stress in independent absolutive pronouns.

3.2.3 Possessive Pronouns

Possession is expressed by apposition and by genitive pronoun suffixes. In apposition the possessor precedes the possessed as in: **daafurs-i min-i** 'Daafursa's house'. Possession can be also expressed by means of genitive pronoun suffixes as in **mine-nke** or 'our house' and **ʔama-ʔya** 'my mother'. The two means to express genitive are not sensitive to proper noun status as exemplified below.

(69) a. **daafurs-i**   **min-i**   **haaro-ho**
       Daafursa-GEN   hoiuse-NOM   new-COP.M
       'Daafursa's house is new.'

    b. **min-i-si**   **haaro-ho**
       house-NOM-his   new-COP.M
       'His house is new.'

The genitive suffix pronouns have the paradigm of the other pronouns.

	Singular			**Plural**	
1st	**-ʔya**	'my'	1st	**-nke**	'our'
2nd	**-kki**	'your (SG)'	2nd	**-ʔne**	'your (PL)'
3rd m.	**-si**	'his'	3rd	**-nsa**	'their'
f.	**-se**	'her'			

3.2.4 Interrogative Pronouns

Five of the Sidaama interrogative pronouns have both absolute and nominative forms.

Absolutive		**Nominative**	
ʔayé/	'whom?'	**ʔay-i**	'who?'
maa/	'what?'	**may-i**	'what?'
hiikkoye	'which'	**hiikk-u**	'which?'
meʔe	'how many/much?'	**meʔ-u**	'how many/much?
maaye-ra	'why?'	**mamaro**[16]	'when?' /**mamoote/**[17] 'when?'

Five which do not distinguish nominative and absolutive are.

---

[16]   **mamaro** 'when' is derived from **mama** 'where?' + **waro** 'time'.

[17]   The word **mamoote** is a derivation from **mama** 'where?' + **wote** 'time' with phonological change.

hiikko	'where?'	hiitto	'how?'
maaye-ra	'why?'	mama	'where?'
mamoote	'when?'		

3.2.5 Relative Pronoun

There are three relative pronoun formatives which are suffixed to verbs: /-h/ 'masculine', /-t/ 'feminine', and /-r/ 'plural'; these are similar to the genitive suffixes for non-attributive pronoun. All relative pronouns, even feminine forms, are case-marked. As elsewhere, the high vowels /-u/ and /-i/ mark nominative.

(70) a. **sirb-annó-*h-u***   **daafursa-ti**
       sing-3SG.M.IMPERF-REL.M-NOM   Daafursa-COP
       'The one (m.) who will sing is Daafursa.'

     b. **sirb-i-tannó-*t-i***   **dančile-ti**
       sing-EE-3SG.F.IMPERF-REL.F-NOM.   Danchile-COP
       'The one who will sing is Danchile.'

     c. **sirb-i-tanno-*r-i***   **daafurs-i-nna**   **dančile-ti**
       sing- EE-3PL.IMPERF-REL.PL-NOM   Daafursa-EE-and   Danchile-COP
       'Those who will sing are Daafursa and Danchile.'

	Relative Suffix	Absolutive relative	Nominative relative
m.	-h	-ha	-hu
f.	-t	-ta	-ti
pl.	-r	-re	-ri

3.2.6 Reflexive Pronouns

The reflexive is based on the word for 'head' **ʔumo** followed by suffixed genitive pronouns.[18] Like other nominal categories, the reflexive may be inflected for case. The absolutive is signaled by stress on the genitive pronoun suffix while the nominative case of reflexives is marked by /-i/ and a destressing of the genitive pronoun suffix.

---

[18] The reflexive construction in Amharic is the exact parallel of Sidaama, also based on the word **ras** 'head' followed by genitive suffixes, and also having an emphatic form in which a personal pronoun precedes the reflexive.

Table 5 Absolutive and Nominative Reflexive Pronouns

Singular	Absolutive Reflexive	Nominative Reflexive	
1ˢᵗ	ʔumo-ʔyá	ʔum-í-ʔya	'myself'
2ⁿᵈ	ʔumo-kkí	ʔum-í-kka	'yourself'
3ʳᵈ M	ʔumo-sí	ʔum-í-sa	'himself'
3ʳᵈ F	ʔumo-sé	ʔum-í-sa	'herself'
Plural			
1ˢᵗ	ʔumo-nké	ʔum-i-nka	'ourselves'
2ⁿᵈ	ʔumo-ʔné	ʔum-i-ʔne	'yourselves'
3ʳᵈ	ʔumo-nsá	ʔum-i-nsa	'themselves'

Sidaama also has an emphatic reflexive which is formed by placing a personal pronoun before a corresponding simple reflexive as in the following examples.

(71) a. ʔan-i   ʔum-i-'ya   kaʔl-ummo
       I-NOM   self-NOM-my   help-1.M.SG.PERF
       'I myself helped.'

b. ninke   ʔum-i-nke   kaʔl-i-nummo
   we.NOM   self-NOM-our   help-EE-1.PL.PERF
   'We ourselves helped.'

3.2.7 Infinitive

An Infinitive is formed by suffixing /-a/ to a verb stem as in **kubb-a** 'to jump/jumping'.
Though the base of an infinitive is verbal, functionally and distributionally it is a nominal and hence it can function either as subject as in (72)a or as object as in (72)b.

(72) a. **dog-a   buša-te**   b. **haʔr-a   hasiʔr-atto**
       cheat-INF bad-COP.F   go-INF   want-2M.SG.IMPERF
       'Cheating is bad.'   'You want to go.'

Infinitives can be subjectless as in (72) or can have subjects which are expressed by a genitive pronoun suffix. Here are a couple of examples with subjects.

(73) a. **t'ook'-a-si   di-bat'oommo**
       flee-INF-his   NEG-like-1MS.PPERF
       'I didn't like his fleeing.'

b. **lotore   k'eel-a-se   mač'č'iš-oommo**

lottery   pass-INF-3FS.GEN   hear-1MS.PPERF
'I have heard of her winning the lottery.'

3.2.8 Negation of Nouns, Pronouns, and Adjectives

Nouns, pronouns, and adjectives are negated by attaching the negative prefix /di-/ 'NEG' to a
noun, a pronoun or an adjective as shown below.

(74) a. **di-ʔanee-ti**   b. **di-mine-ho**   c. **di-worba-ho**
NEG-me-COP   NEG-house-COP.M   NEG-brave-COP.M
'It is not me.'   'It is not a house.'   'He is not brave.'

The morpheme /-**weello**/ has the meaning 'without' and can be attached both to nouns and
pronouns as in **ʔadi-weello** 'without milk' (**ʔado** 'milk') and **ʔani-weello** 'without me'.

3.2.9 Derived Nominals

Sidaama nouns may be derived from verb stems, adjectives, and other nouns. Nevertheless
most of the derived nouns are deverbal. There are four types of nouns which are derived from
verbs. Suffixed to nonhuman nouns /-**aančo**/ derives instruments as in **fey-aančo** 'broom'
(**fey-** 'sweep'), and suffixed to human nouns /-**aančo**/ and /-**aasinčo**/ derive agents as in
ros-aančo 'student' and **ros-iisančo** 'teacher' (**roos-** 'learn, **ros-iis-** 'teach'). Abstract nouns
are derived with /-**(m)ma**/ and /-**(l)le**/ as in **but'ima** 'poverty' (**but'**- 'be poor') and **bat'ille**
'love' (**bat'**- 'love'/'like'). Nominals which indicate country of origin and ethnicity are
derived by the suffixation of /-**aawičča**/ 'm.' ~ /-**aawitte**/ 'f.' and /**tičča**/ 'm.' ~ /**titte**/ 'f.',
respectively, as **ʔamar-tičča/** 'an Amhara man' **Sidan-titte** 'a Sidaama woman'. In addition
to these there are a few other nominalizer suffixes. A few nominals are derived from
adjectives as in **dančimma** from **danča** 'good'/'goodness'.

3.3 Verbs

Verbs are sentence-final, and inflected for tense, aspect, mood, person, number, and, in first
and 2nd-person singular, gender. Sidaama verb stems range from mono-consonantal through
polysyllabic and all end in consonants. Sample verb stems are presented below.

(75) **y**- 'say', **dod**- 'run', **kubb**- 'jump', **dadil**- 'worry', **hamuruurr**- 'be bruised'

3.3.1 Tense/Aspect/Modal

There are five basic or simple tense/aspects having different paradigms of subject-agreement
suffixes: the simple perfect, present perfect, imperfect, imperative/jussive, and converb.
Unlike other Highland East Cushitic languages, the Sidaama perfect, present perfect, and

imperfect distinguish masculine and feminine in the 1st and 2nd person singulars by the suffix-final vowels /-o/ 'm.' and /-a/ 'f.', respectively. For the full paradigms of verb suffixes for the five tense/aspects see Table 6.

The **simple perfect** roughly corresponds to English past tense and expresses a completed action.

(76) **beett-u   hurbaate   ?it-í**
boy-NOM   dinner   eat-3M.SG.PERF
'The boy ate a dinner.'

The **present perfect** expresses events which have happened in the recent past and with recent effect or relevance.

(77) **beett-u   hurbaate   ?it-inó**
boy-NOM   dinner   eat-3M.SG.PPERF
'The boy has eaten a dinner.'

The **imperfect** expresses an incompleted action, whether present or future.

(78) **beett-u   hurbaate   ?it-anno**
boy-NOM   dinner   eat-3M.SG.IMPERF
'The boy eats/will eat a dinner.'

The imperative is for 2nd persons and expresses commands, and **the jussive** (sometimes termed optative) is for 1st and 3rd persons and expresses mood as of 'should, would'. The imperative is marked by the suffixes /-i / 'sg.' and /-e / 'pl.'. In the plural imperative, stem-final single consonants are geminated.

(79) 2nd sg. **sirb-i**   'sing (sg.)!'   **kul-i**   'tell (sg.)!'
2nd pl. **sirb-e**   'sing (pl.)!'   **kul-le**   'tell (pl.)!'

The grammatical significance of stress is evident if one compares the 3rd person m. sg. perfect suffix which is stressed with the 2nd m. sg. imperative suffix which is unstressed. Likewise the 2nd pl. imperative contrasts in stress with the 3 m.sg. converb. The examples below illustrate this contrast.

(80) a. **sirb-í**   'he sang'   (81) a. **sirb-é**   'he having sung'
b. **sírb-i**   'sing (sg.)!'   b. **sírb-e**   'sing (2nd pl./2nd pol.)!'

The imperative of the verb **day-** 'come' has a suppletive form **ʔam-ò** 'come (sg.)!' and **ʔam-mè** 'come (pl.)!'.[19]

The jussive can be viewed as a mild imperative which is inflected for 1st and 3rd persons. The segments in parentheses in the jussive paradigm are optional.

(82) 1^{sg}   **sirb-o**   'let me sing'   1st pl.   **sirb-i-n-o**   'let us sing'

3rd m.   **sirb-o(na)**   'let him sing'   3rd pol. **sirb-i-n-o-(na)** 'let Him sing'

3rd f./pl. **sirb-i-t-o(na)** 'let her/them sing'

The converb is used for all but the main verb in a sequence of verbs, and derives its tense/aspect interpretation from the main verb. The subject of a converb and main verb must be coreferential, as in (83).

(83) **sagale**   **ʔit-é,**   **waa**   **ʔag-í**

     food   eat-1.CVB   water   drink-3MS.PF

     'Having eaten the food, he drank water.'

Table 6 Tense/Aspect Suffixes

	Perfect	Present Perfect	Imperfect	Imperative/ Jussive	Converb
1sg.m	-ummo	-oommo	-eemmo	-o	-é
1sg.f	-umma	-oomma	-eemma		
2sg.m	-itto	-ootto	-atto	-i	-té
2sg.f	-itta	-ootta	-atta		
3 sg.m	-í	-inó	-anno ~ -awo	-o	-é
3sg.f	-tú	-tinó	-tanno ~ -tawo	-to	-té
3pol	-ní	-nonni ~ -nooy	-nanní ~ -nay	-no	-né
1pl	-nummo	-noommo	-neemmo	-no	-né
2pl	-tiní	-tinoonní ~ -tinooy	-tinanní ~ -tinay	-(.)e	-tiné
3pl	-tú	-tinó	-tanno ~ -tawo	-to	-té

---

[19] Suppletion of the imperative of 'come' is a common Ethiopia–wide grammatical feature (see Ferguson *ibid.*, 74). For instance in Amharic the verb **mätt'a** 'come' has the three suppletive forms. **na** 'come (m.sg.)!', **näyi** 'come (f.sg.)!', and **nu** 'come (pl.)!'

The present continuous is a complex form consisting of two parts. In most forms, the first part is a subordinate verb with a continuous suffix /-**anni**/ and the second part consists of a present perfect conjugation of the auxiliary verb /**no-**/ 'be present' for singular persons and /**heed-**/ 'live' + **-no** for 1st and 2nd plural. The paradigm of the present continuous is given below which is based on the verb **sirb-** 'sing'.

Table 7   The Present Contnuous Paradigm

	Continuous form	Present Perfect	
1sg.m	sirb-anni	no-ommo[20]	'I am singing'(M)
1sg.f	sirb-anni	no-oomma	'I am singing' (F)
2sg.m	sirb-i-tanni	no-ootto	'You are singing' (M)
2sg.f	sirb-i-tanni	no-ootta	'You are singing'(F)
3 sg.m	sirb-anni	no	'He is singing'
3sg.f	sirb-i-tanni	no	'She is singing'
3pol	sirb-i-nanni	he?-nonni	'He is singing' (POL)
1pl	sirb-i-nanni	he?-noommo	'We are singing'
2pl	sirb-i-tinanni	heed-dinoonní	'You are singing' (PL&POL)
3pl	sirb-i-tanni	no	'They are singing'

3.3.2 Verb of Presence

The present perfect employs **no-**, while the simple perfect and imperfect employ the other existential verb **heed-** 'live'. The paradigm for the verb of presence can be seen above in Table 6 on the third column. The three forms below exemplify the verb of presence.

(84) a. **no-ommo**   'I am/was present'
    b. **hee?r-eemmo**   'I will live/I live'
    c. **hee?r-ummo**   'I lived'

3.3.3 Verb of possession

Possession in present time is expressed by the verb of presence **no-** 'be present' plus the object suffixes (§3.2.1). In such structures, the possessive noun has no agreement with the possessee. The final /**o**/ of the formative **no-** is lengthened before object suffixes.

(85) a. **farašš-u**   **noo-si**   b. **saa**   **noo-nke**
      horse-NOM   is.present-him   cow   is.present-us

---

[20] The long vowel, i.e. /-**oo**/ of 1st and 2nd person singular is shortened when it occurs after **no-** 'verb of presence', in order to avoid a sequence of three vowels.

'He has a horse.'   'We have a cow.'

3.3.4 Negative Marking in Verbs

The present perfect, imperfect and present continuous share a common negative /di-/. This is the only prefix in Sidaama and one of only two prefixes in HEC languages.[21]

	Affirmative		Negative	
(86) a.	**sirb-oommo**	'I have sung'	**di-sirb-oommo**	'I have not sung'
b.	**sirb-eemmo**	'I sing/shall sing'	**di-sirb-eemmo**	'I do not/shall not sing'

The negative of the present continuous tense is formed by prefixing the negative formative /di-/ to the conjugated forms of the verb of presence, **no-** 'be present' and **heed-** 'live'.

(87) a.	**sirb-anni**	**di-noommo**	'I'm not singing'
b.	**sirb-i-tinanni**	**di-heedd-i-noonni**	'You (pl.) are not singing'

The negative of 2nd sg. imperative is formed by suffixing /-tooti/ while the negative of the 2nd plural has the suffix /-tinoonte/. The negative of all the jussives is formed by suffixing /-nke/.

2nd sg.	**sirb-i-tooti**	'Do not sing (sg.)!'
2nd pl./2nd pol.	**sirb-i-tinoonte**	'Do not sing (pl.)!'
1st	**sirboo-nke**	'let me not sing'

Clauses are negated by the particle /-(i)kki/ which, in fast speech, is shortened to /-kki/ after a verb-final vowel.

(88)	**ʔit-ino-kki**		**daafira,**	**hudiʔr-í**	(fast speech)
	eat-3MS.PPERF-NEG		because	hungry-3MS.PERF	
	'He became hungry because he did not eat.'				

3.3.5 Derived Stems

Verbs may be derived as causatives, reflexives, passives, and reduplicative-intensive. In addition, the suffixes can be combined with one another and result in other derived forms.

3.3.5.1 Causative

---

[21] The only other prefix in HEC languages is the set of genitive pronoun prefixes of Hadiyya (see Hudson in 1976: 258).

There are single and double causatives (factitives). The single causative is formed by adding the suffix /-s/ to a simple verb stem. It is usually added to an intransitive verb stem and the result is a transitive verb.[22] Thus /-s/ could be considered as transitivizer.

(89) **Ledamo,**   **k'aakk'o**   **got'-i-s-í**
Ledamo   baby   sleep-EE-CAUS-3M.S.PERF
'Ledamo made the baby sleep.'

Some transitive verbs (such as **ʔit-** 'eat') can form a causative leading to acquisition of an additional complement.

(90) **Ledamo,**   **k'aakk'o-ho**   **šerko**   **ʔit-i-s-í**
Ledamo   baby-to (m.)   porridge   eat-EE-CAUS-3MS.PERF
'Ledamo fed the baby porridge.'

The double causative (factitive) is suffixed by /-siis/. The factitive is mostly added to transitive verbs such as **ʔit-** 'eat'.

(91) **Ledamo,**   **k'aakk'o**   **šerko**   **ʔit-i-siis-í**
Ledamo   baby   porridge   eat-EE-DBL.CAUS-3MS.PERF
'Ledamo made the baby eat porridge.'

However, there are some intransitive verbs such as **wiʔl-** 'cry/weep' (INTR) which can take the factitive at one go as exemplified below.

(92)   a.   **k'aakk'-u**   **wiʔl- í**
            baby-NOM   cry/weep-3M.SG.PERF
            'The baby cried/wept.'

       b.   **buš-u**   **beett-i**   **k'aakk'o**   **wiʔl-i-šiiš-í**
            bad-NOM   boy-NOM   baby   cry/weep- DBL.CAUS-3M.SG.PERF
            'The bad boy caused the baby to cry/weep.'

Verbs undergo morphological causativization by adding the causative suffixes /-s/ or /-siis/ to their transitive or intransitive bases. In addition, the verb /ʔass-/ 'do/make' expresses causation in a following structure:

(93) **daafurs-i**   **ledamo**   **rosiis-aančo**   **ʔass-í**

---

[22] There are intransitive verbs which also take a double causative. For instance **got'**– 'sleep' can take both the single causative and double causative. Thus the criterion is not strict.

Daafursa-NOM   Ledamo   teach-NMZ   make-3MS.PERF
'Daafursa made Ledamo a teacher.'

3.3.5.2 Reflexive

The reflexive (termed 'autobenefactive' by Hayward (1975) and by Wedekind (in Abebe et.al. 107)) expresses the notion 'for oneself' and is formed by suffixing /-ɗ/ to simple verb stems as in hayšš-i-ɗ- 'wash oneself' (from hayšš- 'wash') as exemplified below.

(94)   beett-u,   ʔalba-si   hayšš-i-ʔr-í   (from /hayšš-i- ɗ-í/)
       boy-NOM   face-3MS.GEN   wash-EE-REFL-3MS.PERF
       'The boy washed his face.'

Even though the reflexive verb seems to be beneficial to the subject of (94), there are other verbs the action of which is detrimental to the subject, for instance in the verb hudiɗ- 'be hungry'. This implies that probably it is better to label these verbs 'reflexive' or 'middle voice' rather than 'autobenefactive'. Verbs such as hudiɗ- 'be hungry' seem to contain the reflexive /-ɗ/ as part of the stem, because there is no verb hud- (there is however the noun hude 'hunger'). Such verbs, lacking a basic stem, are termed 'defective verbs', cf. Amharic adärrägä (Anbessa and Hudson 2007. 73). Reflexives have the potential to license an external "benefactive argument" as in (95).

(95)   guyye,   mine   miʔn-í
       Guyye   house   build.REFL-3MS.PERF
       'Guyye built a house for himself.'

Consider also a parallel sentence without the reflexive -ɗ.

(96)   guyye,   samaago-ra   mine   min-í
       Guyye   Samaago-to   house   build-3MS.PERF
       'Guyye built Samaago a house.'

3.3.5.3 Passive

The suffix /-am/ expresses the passive, usually of transitive verbs.

(97)   hand-u,   hir-am-í
       ox-NOM   sell-PASS-3MS.PERF
       'The ox was sold.'

There are defective passives such as **k'arr-am-** 'be in trouble' without a corresponding transitive base. However, the theoretical basic stem of this verb appears to be **k'arr-** since there is a noun **k'arra** 'trouble'.

3.3.5.4 Intensive (Reduplicative)

The intensive (reduplicative) indicates an action which is repeated several times and is formed by a total reduplication of monosyllabic stems as in **kukkub-**'jump repeatedly' and **kakkad-** 'kick repeatedly' (from **kubb-** 'jump' and **kad-** 'kick'), both with regressive obstruent assimilation (§2.8.3.2).

(98) **beett-u,**   **anga**   **gan-gan-í**
     boy-NOM   hand   beat-INT-3MS.PERF
     'The boy clapped his hands.'

3.3.5.5 Multiple Derivatives

The derived stems can be combined in various ways. Often two derivative suffixes can be combined and in rare cases even three. Examples below are infinitives, suffixed by /**-a**/.

(99) a. /**dun-ɗ-am-a**/
      pour-REFL-PASS-INF
      /**duɗnama**/   (metathesis of **nɗ** to **ɗn**)
      [**duʔnama**] 'to be poured out'   (debuccalaization of /**ɗ**/ to [**ʔ**])

    b. /**ʔit-s-ɗ-a**/
       eat-CAUS-REFL-INF
       /**ʔit-i-s-i-ɗ-a**/   (epenthesis of **i**)
       [**ʔitisiʔra**] 'to feed for one's benefit'   (weakening of /**ɗ**/ to [**ʔr**])

    c. /**k'as-k'as-s-a**/
       stab-INT-CAUS-INF
       /**k'akk'as-s-a**/   (total assimilation of **sk'** to **kk'**)
       [**k'akk'asiisa**] 'to cause a quarrel'   (epenthesis of **ii**)

3.3.6 Compound Verbs

Sidaama has a category of compound verbs the first word of which is specific to the category. The second part is the verb **y-** 'say' in intransitive compounds and **ass-** 'make' in transitive compounds.

<u>intransitive compound</u>   <u>transitive compound</u>

(100) a. **gotti y-í** 'he rose up'   c. **gotti ʔass-í** 'he lifted'
      b. **šikk'i y-í** 'he approached'   d. **šikk'i ʔass-í** 'he brought nearer'

3.3.7 Copula

The copula or be-verb has three grammatically conditioned alternants. /-ho/ 'm. sg.', /-te/ 'f. sg.' and /-ti/, restricted to genitive structures and cleft sentences. Plural forms take either /-ho/ or /-te/, selection between which appears to be arbitrary i.e. a particular noun seems to select either **-ho** or **-te** and the choice appears to be lexically determined. The copula or be-verb does not have a past form.

(101) a. **jomb-i,   ros-aančo-ho**
          Jomba-NOM   learn-AGT-COP.M
          'Jomba is a student.'

   b. **dikkaaše,   busule-te**
       Dikkaashe   clever-COP.F
       'Dikkaashe is clever.'

   c. **kun-i   mine-si-ti**
       this-NOM   house-3SG.GEN-COP
       'This is his house.'

3.4 Adjectives

In Sidaama an adjective precedes the noun as in **lowo faraššo** 'a big horse'. Adjecives like nouns are inflected for gender, number and case as exemplified below.

(102) a. **dur-eessa** 'rich' (m.)   **dur-eette** 'rich'   (f.)
      b. **busule** 'clever' (sg.)   **busul-aadda** 'clever' (pl.)
      c. **busul-u** 'clever' (nom.)   **busule** 'clever' (abs.)

In addition, adjectives agree with their head noun in gender, number and case as shown below.

(103 a. **samaago   dur-eessa-ho**
         Samaago   rich-M-COP.M
         Samaago is rich.'

   b. **dančile   dur-eette-te**
       Danchile   rich-F-COP.F
       Danchile is rich.'

c. **samaago-nna** **dančile** **dur-eyye-te**
Samaago-and Danchile rich-PL-COP.PL
'Samaago and Danchile are rich.'

(104) a. **busule** **beetto** **laʔ-ummo**
clever (ABS) boy/girl see-1MS.PERF
'I saw a clever boy/girl.'

b. **busul-u** **beett-i** **fatana** **saʔ-í**
clever-NOM boy-NOM exam pass-3MS.PERF
'The clever boy passed an exam.'

c. **busule** **beetto** **fatana** **saʔ-ʔú**
clever girl exam pass-3FS.PERF
'The clever girl passed an exam.'

Note that the word **beetto**, under (104 a) being an epicene noun can mean either a boy or a girl when it occurs in object position (§3.1.2). In subject position, however, there is no such ambiguity because if there is a nominative marking then the word will have a masculine menanig while the lack of nominative marking renders it as feminine.

One of the syntactic features specific to adjectives is specification for degree. For instance adjectives are specified for degree lexically by means of the word **lowo geešša** 'very' (*lit.* 'big up to').

(105) **harimo, [lowo geešša] busule-ho**
Harimo big up to clever.ABS-COP.M
'Harimo is very clever.'

A morphological feature which distinguishes adjectives from nouns is their declension for diminutives. Only adjectives take the diminutive /-čč'o/ as in (106).

	Adjective		**Dimunitive**	
(106) a.	**šiima**	'small'	**šiim-i-čč'o**	'tiny'
b.	**faayya**	'beautiful'	**faayy-i-čč'o**	'a little beautiful'

Adjectives can be used either attributively or predicatively. When adjectives function attributively they precede the noun which they modify as in **haaro mine** 'a new house'. This is the expected order since Sidaama is an SOV language. When adjectives are used predicatively, they are followed by a copula such as **-ho** 'is (m.)' or **-te** 'is (f.)' as shown under (107).

(107) a. **beett-u,** **busule-ho** b. **beetto, faayya-te**
boy-NOM clever-COP.M girl beautiful-COP.F
'The boy is clever.' 'The girl is beautiful.'

There are two types of adjective classes: underived and derived. The class of underived adjectives is a very limited one and they form a closed class. According to Dixon (1982: 16) the range of meanings typically conveyed by closed-class adjectives includes words denoting *dimension* (big, small), *color* (black, white), *age* (new, old) , and *value* (good, bad). Sidaama has very few adjectives which express the above meanings and they are listed below.

(108) i. **lowo** 'big' ii. **koliššo** 'black'
    šiima 'small'   **waajjo** 'white'
iii. **haaro** 'new' iv. **danča** 'good'
    akkala 'old'   **buša** 'bad'

Sidaama copes with the shortage of quality-denoting by making use of adjectives derived from stative-inchoative verbs. The formatives which are invoved in this process are **-a**, **-čo** and **-ado**, and their use in particular cases seems to be lexically determined.

	Verb		Adjective	
(109) a.	/buš-/	'become bad'	/buša/	'bad'
b.	/haraʔm-/[23]	'become short'	/harančo/	'short'
c.	/šaal-/	'become thin'	/šaalado/	'thin'

The other strategy used in the formation of adjectives is via relativization of verbs.

(110) **hudiʔr-ino** **mančo**
hungry-3MS.PPERF man
'a hungry person' (lit. 'a person who is hungry')

3.5 Adverbs

Adverbs precede the verbs which they modify as exemplified below.

(111) **waayyiso,** *tewo* **di-ros-anno**
Waayyiso today NEG-learn-3MS.IMPERF
'Waayyiso will not study/learn today.'

The adverbial word class includes expression of time, place, and manner. Three adverbs of

---

[23] The derivation of the reflexive verb **haraʔm–** 'become short' is as follows.
/haram–ɗ/ → /haraɗm–/ → [haraʔm–]

time are **niro** 'last year, **t'a** 'now' and the phrasal adverb **bire waro** 'in past times'. Adverbial functions of manner and place are expressed by means of postpositional phrases or converbs as in (112).

(112) a. **sunuu-nni**   b. **rak-ke**[24]
        slowness-PP   quick-2MS.CONV
        'slowly'   'quickly (you-m.)'

3.6 Postpositions

Sidaama postpositions are divided into free and bound. Free postpositions include **ledo** 'with', **gede** 'like', iima 'on', mule 'near', etc. while the bound postpositions are **-nni** 'from', 'at', 'on', 'by', 'with' as in **min-u-nni** 'from the house' and **sikk'o-te-nni** 'with a stick'.

3.7 Conjunctions

Sidaama has *coordinating* and *subordinating* conjunctions. Coordination is between elements which have the same grammatical status. The coordinating conjunction are **-nna** 'and', **-na** 'interrogative', **-no** 'also/too', **woy** '(either...) or', and **kayni** 'but'.

(113) a. **ʔado,   malawo-nna,   buuro**
        milk   honey-and   butter
        'milk, honey, and butter'

     b. **woy nasse-kki,   woy   wot'e-kki**
        or   soul-your   or   money-your
        'either your soul or your money!'

     c. **ledamo   haʔr-anno.   ʔise--na**
        Ledamo   go-3MS.IMPERF   she-and
        'Ledamo will go. And she?'

     d. **ledamo   haʔr-anno.   ʔise   kayni   di-haɗ-ɗanno**
        Ledamo   go-3MS.IMPERF   she   but   NEG-go-3FS.IMPERF
        'Ledamo will go. But she will not go.'

Subordinating conjunctions integrate a subordinate clause into a main clause and are of three types: complementisers, adverbalizers and relativizers. Complementizers **gede** ~ **-ta** 'that' subordinate a clause as a complement of a main verb. Adverbial subordinators have adverbial

---

[24] The 2nd MS.CONV suffix is /-te/. When it is suffixed to stem-final consonants there is total assimilation. For instance in (91) /rak-te/ becomes [rakke].

functions such as the expression of time, reason, etc. and they always precede the main verb. The list includes the forms -ra 'because', **wote** 'when', **geešša** 'until', **daafira** 'because' and others. The subordinators are exemplified below.

(114) a. **ʔukkuša**   **fatana**   **saʔ-ʔanno**   *gede*   **ʔaf-fino**
     Ukushaa   exam   pass-3fs impf.   that   know-3F.SG.PPERF
     'Ukkusha knows that she will pass the exam.' (**af-fino** < af-tino)

   b. **ʔukkuša**   **fatana**   **saʔ-ʔanno**-*ta*   **ʔaf-fino**
     Ukushaa   exam   pass-3FS.IMPERF-that   know-3F.SG.PPERF
     'Ukkusha knows that she will pass the exam.'

   c. **got'-inó-kki**   *daafira*   **ʔafaaffiʔr-í**
     sleep-3MS.PPERF-NEG   because   yawn-3MS.PERF
     'He yawned because he didn/t sleep.'

   d. **hig-eemmo**   *geešša*   **agar-i-ʔe**
     return-1MS.PER   until   wait-3MS.PERF-1MS.OBJ
     'Wait for me till I return.'

3.8 Discourse Markers

In the preceding sections we have examined all the lexical categories of Sidaama. However, there are some words which do not belong to any of these categories and may be considered to have a discourse (pragmatic) function. Here is a partial list.

(115) a. **ʔee**   'yes'   e. **ballo** 'please!'
   b. **deeʔni** 'no'   f. **hay** 'alas'
   c. **koo**   'you!' (m. vocative)   g. **haššu** 'exclamation of pleasure'
   d. **tee**   'you!' (f. vocative)   h. **eewa** 'yes (strong affirmative)'

The above discourse markers are different from the other lexical categories in that they do not occur as heads or complements, and do not undergo derivation or inflection.

4. Phrasal Categories

4.0 Introduction

The types of phrases in a language depends on the number of lexical categories. This is because a phrasal category is a projection (extension) of its lexical head. Since Sidaama has five lexical categories there are also five corresponding phrasal categories. noun phrase (NP), verb phrase (VP), adjective phrase (AP), adverb phrase (ADVP), and postpositional phrase (PP).

4. 1 Noun Phrase

A noun phrase is a structure which minimally consists of a noun as in **badala-te tima** 'maize bread' (maize-of bread) whereby **tima** 'bread' is the head noun while **badala-te** 'of maize' is a genitive of source. The phrase can be further expanded by adding simple and derived nominal complements. Simple nominal complements include genitive NPs, adjectives and relative clauses. The above NP can be expanded by adding an adjective which serves as a complement to the rest of the phrase as shown below.

(116) **šiima**   [**badala-te**   **tima**]
       small   maize-gen.(m.)   bread
       'a small maize bread'

The number of adjectives is theoretically unlimited. They can be added as needed as the following example demonstrates.

(117) **busule,** **seeda,** **šaalado** **beetto,** **dag-gú**
       clever   tall   thin   girl   come-3FS.PERF
       'The clever, tall, thin girl came.'

Relative clauses are the third type of simple nominal complements.

(118) **hasaaw-u-nna** **hawad-u**   **maant'-onni-re**   **fušš-anno**
       talk-NOM-and winter-NOM hide-IMPRS-REL.PL reveal-3MS.IMPERF
       'A conversation and a winter reveal what is hidden.'

The NP in Sidaama can be further expanded by the addition of various modifiers. These modifiers define the head in terms of time, place, instrument, etc. For instance a temporal adverb together with a genitival /-ti/ can modify the whole NP as in (119).

(119) **tewo-t-i**   [**šiima** [**badala-te**   **tima**]

today-F.GEN-NOM   small   maize-F.GEN   bread
'Today's small maize bread'

In the above structure the locative and the adjective can freely interchange their places indicating that they are found at the same phrasal level.

(120) šiima   [[tewo-t-i   [badala-te   tima]]
      small   today- F.GEN-NOM   maize-gen.(m.)   bread
      'Today's small maize bread'

The basic NP [badala-te tima]] 'maize bread' can be further expanded by adding various specifiers such as a demonstrative, a possessive and a quantifier in that respective order.

(121) [kur-i   ane-ri   lam-u   [[šiimmaadd -u   [badala-te   tima]]]
       these-NOM   my-GEN.PL   two-NOM   small (pl.)-NOM   maize-GEN.F   bread
       'these two small maize breads of mine'

In brief an NP is maximally composed of four elements in the following order: **specifier — modifier(s) — complement(s) — head**. In case of nouns which lack a genitive of source, the elements within an NP are three.

4.2 Verb Phrase

On a semantic basis, Sidaama verbs fall into two classes: *dynamic* and *stative* verbs. The former shows an action while the latter expresses a state, as in the examples.

(122) a. **guyye,**   **waa**   *ʔag-í*
         Guyye   water   drink-3MS.PERF
         'Guyye drank water.'

      b. **guyye,**   **wottadara**   *ʔikk-í*
         Guyye   soldier   become-3MS.PERF
         'Guyye became a soldier.'

Sidaama verbs, in particular dynamic verbs, are classified into *intransitives* and *transitives* based on their selection or non selection of complements.

4.2.1 Intransitives

These verbs usually do not select a complement and include verbs such as **deweeʔl**- 'belch', **mas**- 'be startled' and compound verbs such as **gotti y**- 'stand up'.

(123) a. **waayyiso   deweeʔl-í**   b.   **waayyiso   mas-í**
      Waayyiso   belch-3MS.PERF   Waayyiso   be scared-3MS.PERF
      'Waayyiso belched.'   'Waayyiso was scared.'

Although intransitives do not take NP complements some of them can take PP complements. For instance, the motion verb **had-** 'go' requires a PP complement.

(124) **beett-u,   min-i-ra   haʔr-í**
      boy-NOM   house-EE-to   go-3MS.PERF
      'The boy went home.'

Before discussing the complements which PPs select it may be necessary to clarify the difference between VP₁ and VP₂. If the verb phrase contains two PPs the rightmost PP is the complement of the head verb and together they form VP₁. The rightmost PP on the other hand is the complement of VP₁ and together they form VP₂. Sentence (125) illustrates this point.

(125) **beett-u,   [[makin-u-nni]   [min-i-ra   haʔr-í]]**
                     VP₂   VP₁
      boy-NOM   car-GEN.M-by   home-EE-to   go-3MS.PERF
      'The boy went home by car.'

The selection or non-selection of a PP complement at the level of VP₁ is the main syntactic difference between intransitive verbs of Sidaama. At higher phrasal levels such as VP₂ though, there are no differences. At this level, all intransitive verbs can take various modifiers. Modifiers at the level of VP₂ specify the time, manner, instrument, reason, etc. of the action described by VP₁. In addition, compared to complements of VP₁, adverbial and PP modifiers of VP₂ are optional. This is because such phrases do not describe the action but rather the manner of the action as shown under (126).

(126) **beett-u   bero   makin-u-nni   min-i-ra   haʔr-í**
      boy-NOM   yesterday   car-GEN.M-by   home-EE-to   go-3MS.PERF
      'The boy went home yesterday by car.'

Although a temporal adverb - PP sequence is the default, the reverse order i.e. PP-temporal adverb is also acceptable. The fact that both modifiers can interchange places demonstrates that they are found at the same phrasal level.

Other modifiers within the sentence are sentence adverbials. These are words such as **miteekke** 'perhaps', **halaal-i-nni** 'certainly', **horonta-nni** 'never', etc. They differ from VP adverbials in that they do not describe the VP but rather the certainty, falseness, doubtfulness, etc., of the whole clause. Consequently sentence adverbials do not have a fixed slot within a sentence but can freely move to various positions within a sentence -but not preverbal and not final. Consider (127), in which *miteekke* 'perhaps' is the S-adverb.

(127) a. [*miteekke*   [**beett-u,**   **bero**   **min-i-ra**   **haʔr-inó**]   ]
                    S
       perhaps   boy-NOM   yesterday   home-EE-to   go-3MS.PPERF
       'Perhaps the boy has gone home yesterday.'

     b. [**beett-u,**   *miteekke* [**bero**   **min-i-ra**   **haʔr-inó**]]
       boy-NOM   perhaps   yesterday   home-EE-to   go-3MS.PPERF
       'The boy perhaps has gone home yesterday.'

     c. [**beett-u,**   **bero**   *miteekke*   [**min-i-ra**   **haʔ'r-inó**]]
       boy-NOM   yesterday   yesterday   home-EE-to   go-3MS.PPERF
       'The boy perhaps has gone home yesterday.'

Other grammatical elements which are selected by an intransitive verb at the level of VP$_2$ are specifiers as shown in (127), where a quantifier precedes VP$_2$.

(128) a. [**beett-u,**   *lame hige* [**makin-u-nni**   [**min-i-ra**   **haʔr-í**]]]
         boy-NOM   twice   car-GEN.M-by   home-EE-to   go-3MS.PERF
         'The boy has gone home twice by car.'

4.2.2 Transitives

Transitive verbs require nominal or clausal complements. Depending on the syntactic characteristic of the complement, Sidaama transitives fall into three classes: *semi-transitives*, *mono-transitives*, and *di-transitives*.

Semi-transitive verbs narrowly presuppose their NP complements and thus may have cognate NP complements (such as *šerko* of (129)) or no complements at all.

(129) a. **waaritu,**   *šerko*   **šerk-i-tú**
         Waaritu   porridge   cook porridge-EE-3FS.PERF
         'Waaritu cooked porridge.'

     b. **waaritu,**   **il-tú**
         Waaritu   deliver-3FS.PERF
         'Waaritu gave birth.'

Di-transitives presuppose a beneficiary so typically they take two object NPs: a direct object and an indirect object. Verbs such as **ʔuy-** 'give' and **kul-** 'tell' are examples of di-transitives.

(130) su?nare, k'aakk'o-ho ?ado ?uy-tú
      Su?nare baby-to (m.) milk give-3MS.PERF
      'Su?nare gave milk to the baby.'

In (130) [k'aakk'o-ho] 'to the baby' is an indirect object while ?ado 'milk' is a direct object. This is the preferred default order. Nevertheless the objects can freely interchange their places indicating that both are found at the same phrasal level.

Mono-transitives, with one complement, include verbs such as are. hidɗ- 'buy', ?ag- 'drink', hayšš- 'wash'. In addition, transitives are characterized by their potential for passivization. Transitive verbs can also take clausal complements. *Epistemic* or *conceptual* transitives take finite clauses as their complements and include verbs such as ?af- 'know', 'realize', ?egenn- 'know', mačč'iiš- 'hear'.

(131) ?amalo [[waaritu il-tinó gede] ?af-inó]
      Amalo Waaritu deliver-3FS.PPERF that know-3MS.PPERF
      'Amalo knows that Waaritu has given birth.'

Epistemic verbs have also the potential to select a 'finite infinitival' clause: an infinitive which has a pronominal element, i.e. a genitive suffixed to it. For instance senetence (131) can be rewritten as follows.

(132) ?amalo, [waaritu ?il-a-se ?af-inó]]
      Amalo Waaritu deliver-INF-3FS.GEN know-3MS.PPERF
      'Amalo knows of Waaritu's having given birth.'

Desiderative verbs can take both finite and non-finite (infinitival) clauses. The only desiderative verb in Sidaama is hasiɗ- 'want'.

(133)a. beett-u, [[*loos-a*] hasi?r-anno]
      boy-NOM work-INF want-3MS.IMPERF
      'The boy wants to work.'

   b. beett-u, [[*su?nare loos-sanno* gede] hasi?r-anno]
      boy-NOM Su?nare work-3FS.IMPERF that want-3MS.IMPERF
      'The boy wants Su?nare to work.'

On the other hand the *quotative* verb y- 'say' takes tensed clauses only. For instance, it can occur either with a declarative or an interrogative clause as illustrated below.

(134) beett-u, [["wot'e hasi?r-eemmo"] y-í]

boy-NOM   money   want-1M.SG.IMPERF   say-3MS.PERF
'The boy said "I want money." '

4.2.3 Linking Verbs

Linking verbs are the main representative of eventive verbs and their syntactic function is linking a nominal or an adjectival complement with its subject. Linking verbs of Sidaama consist of two groups. 'verb to be' and 'verb of presence/existence'. The 'verb to be' is /-ho/ ~ /-te/ ~ /-ti/ 'is'. The verbs **ikk-** 'become' and **lab-** 'seem' could be added to this group because syntactically they behave similarly. The 'verb of presence/existence' is **no**. 'Verbs to be' form their VP₁ in conjunction with either an NP or an AP. On the other hand, the 'verb of presence' occurs with NP or PP, in particular a place PP.

(135) a. **Beša,   busule**-te
       Besha   clever-COP.F
       'Besha is clever.'

    b. **yunkur-i   wotadara   ʔikk-í**
       Yunkura-NOM   soldier   become-3MS.PERF
       'Yunkura became a soldier'.

    c. **yunkur-i,   min-u   giddo   no**
       Yunkura-NOM   house-M   inside   exist
       'Yunkura is inside a house.'

4.3 Adjectival phrase

Adjectives, like their nominal and verbal counterparts form their phrasal structure in combination with various complements, modifiers, and specifiers. Depending on their derivational status, adjectives fall into two categories. free and derived. Free adjectives take optional PP complements as shown below.

(136) **marak'e   ʔag-a,   [[k'iida-ho] [danča]]-te**
      soup   drink-INF   cold-for   good-COP.F
      'Drinking soup is good for the cold.'

Adjectives are derived either from nominal or verbal stems. Nominal adjectives form their minimal adjectival phrases (AP₁) without any type of complement as (137) illustrates.

(137) **samaago   busule-ho**
      Samaago   clever-COP.M
      'Samaago is clever.'

At a level of maximal adjectival phrase or AP₂, the adjectives form a maximal AP together with PPs as shown under (138).

(138) **dančile**   [*laʔlama-se   gede*   **busule**]-te
       Danchile   aunt-her   like   clever-COP.F
       'Danchile is clever like her aunt.'

An AP₂ can be formed in conjunction with a *comparative* structure. The comparative involves NP₂-**nni** which is followed by an optional **roor-e** 'more' (lit. 'exceed'-CNV). An adjectival phrase that involves a comparative is exemplified below.

(139) **bat'iso**, [**baado-nni**   (**roor-e**)   [**bareeda**]]-ho
       Bat'iso   Baado-from   (more-CNV)   courageous-COP.M
       'Bat'iso is more courageous than Baado.'

The other element which adjectives select is a specifier. For instance the quantifier **lowo geešša** 'very much' can be added at the beginning of sentence (140) and the AP can attain its maximal extension.

(140) **dančile,**   **lowo geešša** [*la'lama-si*   *gede*   **busule**]-**te**
       Danchile   very much   ⁃ aunt-3MS.GEN   like   clever-COP.F
       'Danchile is very clever like her aunt.'

4.4 Adverbial Phrase

Adverbial functions are expressed by "true" adverbs such as **niro** 'last year'or **tayt'e** 'this year'. In addition, it is expressed by other categories such as a PP **sunuu-nni** 'slowly'or converbs such as **rah-e** 'quickly'. Adverbs do not have complements. Hence they form their minor adverbial phrase (ADVP₁) on basis of their heads alone as (141) illustrates.

(141) **geerč-u**,   [**sunuu-nni**]   **haʔr-í**
       old:man-nom.   slow-ADV   go-3MS.PERF
       'The old man went slowly.'

At higher phrasal level let say at the level of ADVP₂, adverbials form their phrases from PPs such as [**k'učč-u gede**] 'like a tortoise' and a specifier such as [*lowo geešša*] 'very' as example (142) demonstrates.

(142) **geerč-u**,   [**k'učč'-u**   **gede** [*lowo   geešša* [**sunuu-nni**]]   **haʔr-anno**
       old:man-NOM   tortoise-M   like   very much   slow-ADV   go-3MS.IMPERF
       'The old man goes very slowly like a tortoise.'

4.5 Postpositional Phrase

Postpositions are function words which occur usually with NPs. The following is a list of the main postpositions of Sidaama.

(143) a. **-ra** 'to' c. **gede** 'like' e. **/iima/** 'on'
      b. **-nni** 'from' d. **geešša** 'up to' f. **/ledo/** 'with'

Postpositions can occur with NPs and simple clausal structures. Examples are provided for some of the PPs listed in (143).

(144) a. **fullaas-i-***ra*
    Fullaasa-EE.M-to
    'to Fullaasa'

    b. **fullaas-i-***nni*
    Fullaasa-EE.M-from
    'from Fullaasa'

    c. **goww-u**   **beett-i**   *gede*
    foolish-NOM   boy-NOM   like
    'like a foolish boy'

    d. **ʔirb-u**   **katam-i**   *geešša*
    Irba-GEN.M   city-NOM   up to
    'up to the town of Irba'

In each example the italicized item on the right hand side is a postposition and it forms the head of the constituent while the leftmost element is its complement. What was presented above is a simple PP structure. Consider sentences below which contain PPs with their nominal complements.

(145) a. **[beša,**   **[[min-i-ra]**   **haɗ-ɗú]]**
    Besha   home-E -to   go-3FS.PERF.
    'Besha went home.'

    b. **[beša,**   **[[ʔama-se]**   **[ledo]]**   **haɗ-ɗú]**
    Besha   mother-her   with   go-3FS.PERF
    Besha went with her mother.'

There are a number of PPs which can occur in combination with other PPs. In such instances the sentence carries a metaphorical connotation as shown below.

(146) **beett-u,**   **[[k'ult'u'me-te gede]** **[way-i**   **giddo]]**   **hos-anno**
    boy-NOM   fish-GEN.F   like   water-NOM   in   spend day-3MS.IMPERF
    'The boy spends the day inside water like a fish.' (i.e. 'he bathes frequently')

4.6 Complex Phrases

A simple phrase consists of a single lexical head while a complex one consists of a lexical head plus complements and/or specifiers. Sidaama has nominal, verbal and adjectival complex phrases.

4.6.1 Complex Noun Phrase

Complex NPs are NPs which contain a clausal complement or any type of modifier complements. One of these complements is an infinitival clause. Consider the following example with such a clause.

(147) [[**turbo-t-i**   **k'olč-anšo**   **k'eel-a-te**]   *yorto*]
       Turbo-of-F.GEN--NOM   outrace-NMZ   win-INF-GEN.F.SG   wish
       'Turbo's wish to win the race'

The structure [**Turbo-ti   k'olč-anšo   k'eel-a-te**] 'Turbo's race winning' is a nonfinite infinitive clause which functions as a clausal complement for the head noun [**yorto**] 'wish'. NPs can take also relative clause complements as shown under (148).

(148) [**?amalo**   **hir-anno(-h-u)**   [**hand-i**]]
       Amalo   sell-3MS.IMPERF(-REL-NOM)   ox-nom
       'The ox that Amalo will sell'

In the above structure the verb **hir-anno** 'he will sell' is relativized by the suffix /-h/ '3M.SG.REL'. In such structures the relative markers are optional as is indicated by the parentheses. In addition, there is a restriction regarding the tense/aspect choice of the relativized verb: it occurs either in present perfect or in imperfect and never in perfect.

In subject position, however, the relative suffixes are obligatory.

(149) **loos-anno-ikki-h-u,**   **di-?it-anno**
       work-3 M.SG.IMPERF-NEG-REL.M-NOM-nom.   NEG-eat-3M.IMPERF
       'One who doesn't work will not eat.'

In the previous examples we have seen relatives formed on basis of transitive verbs such as **hir-** 'sell'. In Sidaama intransitives can be relativized as (150) below demonstrates.

(150) **jomb-i**   **got'-inó-t-i**   **got'-ano**
       Jomba-NOM   sleep-3MS.PPERF-that   sleep-NMZ
       'The sleep which Jomba slept'

There is a discernible difference between a relativized transitive and intransitive. When an intransitive verb is relativized, the noun which accompanies it is a cognate i.e. they share the same verb stem. Relativizaion is not restricted to object NPs alone. A subject NP can be relativized too as the example in (151b) below demonstrates. First consider the simple sentence in (151a) and then its relativized counterpart in (151b).

(151) a. [beett-u,   [ʔanna-si   kaaʔl-í]]
        boy-NOM   father-his   help-3MS.PERF
        'The boy helped his father.'

    b. [[ʔanna-si   kaaʔl-inó]   beett-i]
       father-his   help-3MS.PPERF   boy-NOM
       'The boy who helped his father'

The other grammatical element which can be relativised is a dative object as shown under (152) where (152a) is a basic sentence and (152b) is its relativised counterpart.

(152) a. suʔnare   [mančo-te]   mitt'aššo   ʔuy-tinó]]
        Su'nare   woman-for   griddle   give-3FS.PPERF
        'Su'nare gave to the woman a griddle.'

    b. suʔnare   [mitt'aššo   ʔuy-tinó-se]   [mančo]]
       Su'nare   griddle   give-3FS.PPERF-her   woman
       'the woman to whom Su'nare gave a griddle'

4.6.2 Complex Verb Phrase

Simple VPs minimally consist of a head verb which is optionally preceded by complements or modifiers as (132) below demonstrates.

(153)   beett-u,   min-i-ra   haʔr-í
        boy-NOM   house-EE-to   go-3MS.PERF
        'The boy went home.'

Complex VPs on the other hand consist of clausal complements or modifiers as shown under sentence (154).

(154) [beett-u,   [yot-i   min-i-ra   haʔr-ino   gede]   ʔaf-inó]
      boy-nom.   Yota-nom.   home-EE-to   go-3MS.PPERF   that   know-3MS.PPERF
      'The boy knows that Yota went home.'

The above sentence consists of the complementiser [gede] 'that' and the embedded clause [yot-i min-i-ra haʔr-inó] 'Daafursa went home'. The function of the complementizer [gede] is signalling that the embedded clause is the complement of the verb [ʔaf-inó] 'he knows'.

A minor verbal phrase in combination with adverbial clauses forms the major VP as shown under (155).

(155) bett-u,   [ʔanni-si   ʔuddano hiʔranno-si-h-u-ra]   hagiiʤ-í
       boy-NOM   father-his cloth   buy-him-REL-NOM-for   please-3MS PERF
       'The boy was pleased because his father will buy him a cloth.'

The complement and modifier clauses which we have seen above are verbals. In Sidaama nominals too can function as complements of major VPs. The nominals which usually fulfill this task are infinitives as shown below.

(156) a. beett-u,   [[don-i   hando   hiʤ-a-si]   ʔaf-inó]
         boy-NOM   Dona-NOM   ox   buy-INF-his know-3MS.PPERF
         'The boy knows Dona's buying of an ox.'

      b. manč-u,   [__ hando   hiʤ-a(-ra)]   hasiʔr-anno
         man-NOM   ox   buy-INF (to)   want-3MS.IMERF
         'The man wants to buy an ox.'

In (156a) the clause [don-i   hando hihiʤ-a-si] 'Daafursa's buying of an ox' contains the finite infinitive [hiʤ-a-si] 'his buying'. The suffix which is attached to the infinitive form of the verb, /-si/ 'his', marks a 3M.SG subject [dona]. In (156b) on the other hand, the clause [__ hando hiʤ-a] 'to buy an ox' contains [hiʤ-a] 'to buy' which is a non-finite infinitive. This is because [hiʤ-a] does not have any formative to mark the subject and hence this lack of subject is indicated by the long dash. In both examples of (156) the infinitives function as complements to the head verbs. In (156a) the epistemic verb ʔaf- 'know' takes a finite infinitive complement while in (156b) the desiderative verb hasiʤ- 'want' takes a non finite infinitive complement.

4.6.3 Complex Adjectival Phrases

Adjectival phrases, like their verbal and nominal counterparts, have complex forms which they build in combination with clauses. Consider the following example.

(157) ʔane-nni   roor-u   jawaati,   da-anno   (Luc. 3. 16)
      me-from   more-nom.   Powerful   come-3MS.IMPERF
      'One more powerful than me will come.'

In Sidaama the concept *more* or *superior* is conveyed by the word **roore** 'more', which is the gerundive form of **roor-** 'excel'. This verb in conjunction with the PP **ʔane-nni** 'than me' functions as a comparative adjective.

Sentence (157) is not the only way for expressing comparative of adjectives. The second alternative whereby the comparative word is rendered by means of a relativized form of the verb **/roor-/** 'excel' as illustrated below.

(158) **ʔane-nni   roor-inó(-h-u)   jawaati],   da-anno**
       me-from   excel-3MS.PPERF-REL-M   powerful   come-3MS.IMPERF
       'One more powerful/brave than I will come.'

In (158) the comparative clause in conjunction with the adjective [**jawaati**] forms a subordinate clause. This subordinate clause in turn functions as a modifier of the main clause. The comparative clause is subordinated by the relative formative /-**h-u**/ which is optional.

Sidaama makes use of the postposition **geešša** 'up to, like' plus the verbs **roor-** 'excel'and **ʔaj-** 'be less' to express various degrees of comparison. Thus, **geešša** expresses equality, **roor-** expresses superiority and **ʔaj-** expresses inferiority. Of the three only **geešša** 'equal' can be combined with an AP for purposes of comparison. Of the two verbs only **roor-** 'excel' is used to express both the sense of superiority or inferiority as shown below.

(159) a. [[**hawaas-u   geešš-i]   halaʔlad-i]**
           Awasa-GEN.M   up to-NOM   wide-NOM
           'a lake as wide as Hawaasa'

      b. [[**bat'iso   roor-inó]   worb-i]**
           Bat'iso   excel-3MS.PPERF   brave-NOM
           'one who is braver than Bat'iso'[1]

      c. [[**ʔargat-i-nni   roor-inó]   goww-i]**
           Argata-GEN.M-from   excel-3MS.PPERF   foolish-NOM
           'one who is more foolish than Argata'

5.0 Sentence Structure

On the basis of clause types, Sidaama sentences are divided into two: simple and complex. Simple sentences consist of a single main clause while complex ones comprise one or more subordinate clauses, in addition to a main clause. Simple sentences are formally classified into three syntactic types: *declarative*, *interrogative*, and *imperative*. Each sentence type is correlated with a specific discourse function.

5.1 Declarative Sentence

A declarative is used in the expression of statements and it comprises four types of sentences: eventive, stative, active, and passive.

5.1.1 Eventive Sentences

Eventive sentences describe the state, quality, or manner of the subject of the sentence. Such sentences contain the copulatives /-ho/ ~ /-ti/ ~ /-te/ 'is', the inchoative verb ʔikk-'become', and the verb **lab-** 'seem'. Eventive senetnces are syntactically similar in that their verbs require a nominal or an adjectival complement which is linked to its external argument as exemplified under (160).

(160) a. **dangiso,   ros-aančo-***ho*
        Dangiso   learn-NMZ-COP.M
        'Dangiso is a student.'

    b. **bayriid-i   beett-i-kki,   ʔan-i,   ʔesawu-ti**
        elder-NOM   son-NOM-your   I-NOM   Esau-COP.M
        'I am your eldest son Esau.'

    c. **dangiso,   ros-iis-aančo   ʔikkk-í**
        Dangiso   learn-CAUS-NMZ   become-3MS.PERF
        'Dangiso became a teacher.'

    d. **ʔargat-i,   gowwa   law-anno**
        Argata-NOM   foolish   seem-3MS.IMPERF
        'Argata seems to be foolish.'

5.1.2 Stative Sentences

Stative sentences describe the state of their subject as shown below.

(161) a. **hoors-i,   duʔm-í**

      Hoorsa-NOM   become fat-3MS.PERF
      'Hoorsa became fat.'

  b. **hoors-i,**   **jaaw-í**
      Hoorsa-NOM   become thin-3MS.PERF
      'Hoorsa became thin.'

The verbs in (161) i.e. **duʔm-** 'become fat' and **jaaw-** 'become thin' are called stative because their function is describing the state of the subject. A syntactic feature of stative verbs is their non-selection of complements. Another feature of a stative verb such as **duʔm-** 'become fat' is the fact that it has a corresponding adjective **duʔma** 'fat'.

Sentences which involve 'eventive' verbs can also be included under stative sentences because syntactically they are similar in that they do not select complements. Sentences under (141) illustrate this fact.

(162) a. **daafurs-i,**   **hagiidʼd-í**
      Daafursa-NOM   become happy-3MS.PERF
      'Daafursa became happy.'

  b. **woš-i-čč-u,**   **dut-í**
      dog-EE-SGV-NOM   bark-3MS.PERF
      'The dog barked.'

5.1.3 Active Sentences

Simple sentences outside the class of statives and eventives belong to active sentences. Such sentences contain verbs which denote a certain action as in (163).

(163) **beša,**   **min-i-ra**   **hadʼ-dú**
      Besha   house-EE-to   go-3FS.PERF
      'Besha went home.'

Other sentences contain verbs which express the action which the subject performs on external objects as in (164).

(164) **dančile,**   **ʔooso-se-ra**   **sagale**   **ʔuy-tú**
      Danchile   children-her-to   food   give-3FS.PERF
      'Danchile gave food to her children.'

All the sentences which we have seen above have a specific personal subject. However, there are also 'subjectless' sentences which contain an impersonal subject. Furthermore, Sidaama does not have a separate verb form for an impersonal subject. Instead this function is fulfilled by **-nanni**, an impersonal marker which is identical in shape to a 3rd polite imperfect marker. Consider the following examples.

(165) a. **geerra,   mačč'iš-i-nanni**
elders   listen-EE-IMPRS
'One listens to elders.'

    b. **magano,   waajj-i-nanni**
God   fear-EE-IMPRS
'One fears God.'

As can be seen a feature which distinguishes sentences with impersonal subjects from sentences with regular subjects is that their tense/aspect is always in imperfect form.

5.1.4 Passive Sentences

Passive sentences contain a subject which is the recipient of the action denoted by the verb. Passive sentences of Sidaama are indicated by a passive suffix /-am/. By their very nature, only transitive verbs can have passive forms.

(166) a. **mat'aaf-u   moor-am-inó**
book-NOM   steal-PASS-3MS.PPERF
'The book was stolen.'

    b. **hand-u   hir-am-inó**
ox-NOM   sell-PASS-3MS.PPERF
'The ox was sold.'

5.1.5 Negative Sentences

A negative of an independent clause is marked by the negative prefix **di-** 'not' while the negative of relatives and subordinate clauses is **-ikki** as illustrated below.

(167) a. **ʔarfaaso,   qamise   di-hidd-i-tannno**
Arfaaso   dress   NEG-buy-EE-3FS.IMPERF
'Arfaaso will not buy a dress.'

    b. **rewo   hendonni-ikki   wote   ʔiill-i-tanno**
death   be aware-neg   when   arrive-EE-3FS.IMPERF
'Death arrives unexpectedly.'

c. **los-anno-ikki-h-u**   **di-ʔit-anno**
work-3MS.IMPERF-*NEG*-REL-NOM   NEG-eat-3MS.IMPERF
'One who doesn't work will not eat.'

Negation is not necessarily always indicated by means of negative morphemes. The verbs **gat-** 'remain' and **hoog-** 'be unable' convey the concept of negation as shown under (168).

(168) a. **man-č-u,**   **but'iččo**   **ʔikk-e**   **gat-í**
          man-SGV-NOM   poor   be-3MS.CVB   remain-3MS.PERF
          'The man remained poor.'

       b. **beett-u,**   **fatana**   **saʔ-a**   **hoog-í**
          boy-NOM   exam   pass-INF   unable-3MS.PERF
          'The boy was unable to pass the exam.'

There is an additional negative formative **hiʔnoonti** 'no' which functions as a disapproval word when one gives an incorrect answer to a Sidaama riddle known as **hibbo.**[25] If the person being asked solves the riddle correctly, then the one who posed the riddle approves it by uttering **ʔee** 'yes' or **ʔaf-ootto** 'you know (got) it' and **hiʔnoonti** 'no' if he fails to solve the riddle. An example of the **hibbo** riddle is given in (148) below where speakers A and B are indicated by the respective letters.

(169) A. **hibbo!**
          'a riddle'
       B. **hibibbi!**
          'O.K. proceed with your riddle.'

       A. **ʔabb-i-ʔya**   **beetto**   **hig-i-hu**   **saʔ-i-hu**   **sunk'-anno**[26]
          uncle-EE-my   daughter   returns-REL   pass-REL   kiss-3MS.IMPERF
          'Every passerby kisses my uncle's daughter.'

       B. **k'aakk'o-ho**
          infant-COP.M.
          'It is an infant.'

---

[25] The Sidaama *hibbo* is the equivalent of the Amharic riddle/puzzle known as **ənqoqəlləš.**

[26] Sidaama has two separate lexemes for the English word 'uncle'. **ʔabbo** 'a maternal uncle' and **wosiila** 'a paternal uncle'.

A. **hi?noonti**
    'No' (it is not a correct answer).

B. **gaaya-ho**
    tobacco pipe-COP.M.
    'It is a tobacco pipe.'

A. **?af-ootto**
    know-2.M.SG.PPERF
    'You knew (got) it.'

5.2 Interrogative Sentences

Interrogatives comprise *content questions, Yes-No questions*, and *alternative questions*. In addition to the major question types there are also the minor classes of *rhetorical* and *echo* questions.

5.2.1 Content Questions

Content questions involve the use of question words which usually precede the predicate. Consider (170) where the question words are italicized.

(170) a. **tewo,   dikko** *hiiko*   **nó?**
          today   market where   present
          'Where is the market today?'

b. **?at-i,**   *?ayé*   **beettoo-ti** ?[27]
    you-NOM   *whose*   child-COP
    'Whose child are you?'

c. **tewo   dikko-te**   *maa*   **hir-ootto?** [28]
    today   market-at   *what*   sell-2MS.PPERF
    'What have you sold today at the market?'

---

[27] The copula **–ti** has an interesting phonological feature. Almost all nouns which end in short vowel lengthen their vowel before **–ti**. Consider the following examples.
a. **?anee–ti**   (the basic form is **?ane** 'me').
    me–is
    'It is I.'
b. **ninke   magan–u   ?oosoo–ti**   (the basic form is **?ooso** 'children')
    we   God–gen(m.)   children–are
    'We are the children of God.'

    d. *me?e*   **saate-ti?** [29]
       how much   hour-COP
       'What time is it?' (*lit*. What is the hour?')

    e. *maaye-ra*   **keešš-ootto?**
       what-for   be late-2MS.PPERF
       'Why are you late?'

There are two question words for 'where': **mama** and **hiikko**. The same applies to 'when' which is expressed by the question words **mamoote** and **mamaro**.[30] However, there is a distinct semantic difference between **mamoote**, used for an event which has happened relatively recently, and **mamaro**, which refers to events that took place many years ago. The following sentences exemplify the difference.

(171) a. *mamoote*   **ha?r-atto?**
       when   go-2M.SG.IMPERF
       'When will you go?' (could be within a few hours or days)

      b. **t'alyaanu,** **top'iya**   *mamaro*   **k'as-í?**
        Italians   Ethiopia   when   invade-3M.SG.PERF
       'When did the Italians invade Ethiopia?'

In the next section we will investigate sentence elements which can be questioned. Sidaama permits the questioning of a clause, a phrase, or a lexical item within a given sentence. First consider the following declarative sentence.

(172) [**guyye,** [[**rodii-si**   **ledo**] [**sikk'o-te-nni**]]   [**hamaššo**]   **š-í**]]]
      Guyye   brother-his with stick-GEN.F-with snake   kill-3M.SG.PERF
      'Guyye killed a snake with a stick [together] with his brother'

The phrasal components of the sentence under (172) are the following ones. The NPs are [**guyye**] 'Guyye' which is a subject and [**hamaššo**] 'snake' which is an object. The PPs on the other hand are [**rodii-si ledo**] 'with his brother' and [**sikk'o-te-nni**] 'with a stick'. The VP is [**rodii-si ledo sikk'o-te-nni hamaššo š-í**] 'he killed a snake with a stick (together) with his brother'. Each of the above phrases can be questioned. First consider how the two NPs can be questioned.

---

[28] In fast speech **maa** 'what?' is shortened to **ma**.

[29] The Sidaama word [**saate**] is a loan from the Amharic **sä'at** 'hour'.
[30] The question word **mamoote** appears to be derived from **mama** 'where' + **wote** 'time'. Similarly **mamaro** is presumably derived from **mama** 'where' + **waro** 'time'.

(173)a. *ʔay-i*   **rodii-si**   **ledo** **sikk'o-te-nni**   **hamaššo** **š-í**
       who-NOM brother-his with stick-GEN.F-with snake   kill-3MS.PERF
       'Who killed a snake with a stick together with his brother?'

    b. **guyye,** **rodii-si**   **ledo** **sikk'o-te-nni**   *maa* **š-í**
       Guyye   brother-his with stick-GEN.F-with *what* kill-3MS.PERF
       'What did Guyye kill with a stick together with his brother?'

In sentence in (173a) the subject NP is questioned while in (173b) what is questioned is the object NP. Note that the place where the question word appears in (173) is the same as the place which is occupied by a subject NP and an object NP in the declarative sentence (174).

The following questions can be posed regarding the PPs.

(174) a. **guyye** *ʔayé* *ledo* **sikk'o-te-nni**   **hamaššo** **š-í**?
       Guyye *whom* with stick- GEN.F-with snake   kill-3MS.PERF
       '*With whom* did Guyye kill a snake with a stick ?'

    b. **guyye** **rodii-si**   **ledo** *maay-i-nni*   **hamaššo** **š-í**?
       Guyye brother-his with *what*- GEN.M-*with* snake   kill-3MS.PERF
       '*With what* did Guyye kill a snake together with his brother?'

The VP can be questioned by means of the interrogative pronoun together with the verb **ass-** 'do' in the following way.

(175)   **guyye,** *maa* **ʔass-í**
       Guyye *what* do-3MS.PERF
       'What did Guyye do?'

All the interrogative sentences which we have seen above involve lexical verbs. Now let us see how sentences with *linking* and *existential* verbs can be questioned. First consider simple sentences with *linking* and *existential* verbs in (176a) and (176b), respectively.

(176) a. **suʔnare,** **kawiiččo** **nó**
       Suʔnare here   present
       'Suʔnare is here.'

    b. **suʔnare,** **dureette** **ʔikk-i-tú**
       Suʔnare rich   become-3FS.PERF
       'Suʔnare became rich.'

The above sentences can be questioned in the following way.

(177) a. **suʔnare,** *hiikko* **nó**
Suʔnare a where present
'Where is Suʔnare?'

b. **suʔnare,** *maa* **ʔikk-i-tú**
Suʔnare what become-3FS.PERF
'What did Suʔnare become?'

In all the above examples simple interrogatives were examined. Below we will consider complex interrogatives which involve two or more question words. For instance two or more questions can be posed for various phrases within sentence (178).

(178) a. *ʔay-i,* *maa* *ʔass-í* (questions **Subject NP** and **VP**)
who-NOM what do-3MS.PERF
'*Who* did *what*?'

b *ʔay-i,* *ʔayé* *ledo,* **hamaššo** **š-í** (questions **Subject NP** and **PP₁**)
who-NOM whom with snake kill-3MS.PERF
'*Who with whom* killed a snake? '

c. *ʔay-i,* *maa,* *may-nni,* **š-í** (questions **NP, object NP** and **PP₂**)
who-NOM what what-with kill-3MS.PERF
'*Who* killed *what with what*?'

As example (178) demonstrates various elements within a sentence can be questioned. These include subject NP, object NP, VP or modifier PPs. The order of the interrogative pronouns in complex interrogative clauses reflects their within a declarative sentence.

5.2.2 Yes-No Questions (*ee-dee'ni* Questions)

In Sidaama there are questions which are termed *yes-no (ʔee - dee'ni)*. These questions are classified into three sub-types. *positive Yes-No questions, negative Yes-No questions,* and *tag questions.*

5.2.2.1 Positive Yes-No Questions

A positive Yes-No question is formed in two ways. The first one involves suffixing the interrogative **-ni** to a declarative sentence and the second involves raising the final intonation of a declarative sentence. Positive Yes-No questions are *non-conducive* in Sidaama i.e. they do not indicate whether the speaker expects a certain kind of answer.

(179) Speaker A.   **gaʔʔa**   **k'aʔe-ra**   **haʔr-atto-ní/haʔr-attó**
                  tomorrow home-to   go-2MS.IMPERF-Q
                  'Will you go home tomorrow?'

        Speaker B.   **ʔee,**   **haʔr-eemmo**
                  'yes   go-1M.SG.IMPERF
                  'Yes I shall go.'

5.2.2.2 Negative Yes-No Questions

Negative Yes-No questions are formed by means of the negative prefix **di-** 'not' as (180) exemplifies.

(180) **godoʔl-a**   **di-hasiʔr-atto?**
       play-INF   NEG-want-2MS.IMPERF
       'Don't you want to play?'

Using a negative construction can turn a Yes-No question into a reprimand or mild reproof. Such kind of structure has two parts. The first part is an imperative and the second part consists of a negative sentence to which -**he**, a 2nd sg.m. object suffix is attached.

(181) **mat'aafa**   **abbi-i**   **di-y-uummo-he?**
       book   bring-2MS.IMP   not-say-1M.SG.PF-you
       'Didn't I tell you to bring a book?'

5.2.3 Tag Questions

A tag question is composed of a Yes-No interrogative to which a question particle -**ni** is suffixed. There are two types of tag questions: positive and negative. Sidaama tag questions have a polarity which is not observed in other types of questions. This means a positive clause takes a negative tag and vice versa. Example (182) demonstrates this.

(182) a. **beett-u,**   **di-sirb-anno.**   **sirb-anno-nni?** (positive tag)
          boy-NOM NEG-sing-3MS.IMPERF   sing-3MS.IMPERF-Q
          'The boy will not sing. Will he?'

      b. **beett-u,**   **sirb-anno.**   **di-sirb-anno?** (negative tag)
          boy-NOM   sing-3MS.IMPERF   NEG-sing-3MS.IMPERF
          'The boy will sing. Won't he?'

5.2.4 Alternative/Disjunctive Questions

Sidaama has an interrogative known as an *alternative/disjunctive* and which is marked by the suffix **-nso** 'or'. It is formed by connecting a cleft sentence with an interrogative clause by means of the alternative question marker **-nso** 'or'.

(183) **da-atto-h-u**   **ʔattee-ti-***nso* **wole**   **ʔagadɗ-inó?**[31]
       come-2MS.IMPERF-REL   you-is-or   other   wait-1PL.JUSS
       'Are you the one who is coming or should we wait for another one?'

(184) **loos-a-***nso*   **foolišši?r-a**   **hasi?r-atto?**
       work-INF-or   rest-INF   want-2MS.IMPERF
       'Do you like to rest or to work?'

A contrast between a positive and a negative form of the same sentence can be achieved when such two sentences are conjoined **-nso** as in (164) below.

(185) **ha?r-atto-***nso*   **di-ha?r-atto?**
      go-2MS.IMPERF-or   NEG-go-2MS.IMPERF
      'Do you go or don't you?' (*lit.* 'Do you go or don't you go?')

Where there are more than two conjuncts, the alternative **–nso** is always suffixed to the penultimate conjunct.

(186) **loos-atto**   **godo?l-atto-***nso*   **got'-atto?**
      work-2MS.IMPERF   play-2MS.IMPERF-or   sleep-2MS.IMPERF
      'Do you work, play or sleep?'

In Sidaama any constituent can be made into an alternative question. A couple of examples illustrate this point.

(187) a. **hando-nso**   **saa**   **hidɗ-itto**   (nominal object)
         ox-or   cow   buy-2MS.PERF
         'Did you buy a cow or an ox?'

      b. **kawiiččo-nso**   **hakkiiččo**   **?ofoll-atto**   (locative adverbial)
         here-or   there   sit-2MS.IMPERF
         'Will you sit here or there?'

---

[31] The underlying form of the verb 'come' appears to be /**dag**-/. This is because in 3F.SG.PERF form we have **dag-gú** (from **dag-** + **tú**). However, the final /**g**/ of this verb stem is a unique one because it is unstable. It is deleted before vocalic-initial suffixes. If the deletion leads to sequences of two different vowels then an epenthetic **y** or **w** are inserted.Consider the examples below where /-**i**/ marks 3M.SG.PERF and /-**ummo**/ 1M.SG.PERF.
a. /dag-í/   → /da-í/   (deletion of g) →   [**dayí**]   'he came' (epenthesis of **y**)
b. /dag-ummo/   → /da-ummo/   (deletion of g) →   [**dawummo**] 'I came' (epenthesis of **w**)

c. **suuk'e**   **ʔalba-nni-nso**   **baɗɗe-nni**   **no**   (place adverbial)
   shop   front-POST-or   back- POST   present
   'Is the shop at the front or at the back?'

5.2.5 Echo Questions

Sidaama echo questions involve the echoing of a statement. They have an intonation pattern which is marked by a gradual rise over the last part of the sentence as exemplified below.

(188) Speaker A.   **hando**   **hidɗ-ummo**
              ox   buy-1MS.PERF
              'I bought an ox'.

      Speaker B.   **hando**   **hidɗ-uummo?**
              ox   buy-1MS.PERF
              'I bought an ox?'

In Sidaama, the yes-no echo question of speaker B is identical with the statement made by speaker A.[32] A yes-no echo question is not the only option for speaker B. For instance he can also use a content echo question as in (189).

(189) Speaker A.   **hando**   **hidɗ-ummo**
              ox   buy-1MS.PERF
              'I bought an ox'

      Speaker B.   **maa**   **hidɗ-ummo?**   (with rising intonation on **maa** 'what?')
              what   buy-1MS.PERF
              'I bought a what?'

Imperatives too can be echoed. Compare the sentence given below.

---

[32] The same situation holds for Amharic regarding echo questions. The statement of Speaker A and the echo question of Speaker B are exactly the same as illustrated in the example below.
Speaker A.   **bäre**   **gäzza–hu**
          ox   buy–1m pf.
          'I bought an ox.'
Speaker B.   **bäre**   **gäzza–hu** ?   (with rising intonation)
          ox   buy–1m pf.
          'I bought an ox?' (*lit.* 'I bought an ox?')
This could be a pan–Ethiopian linguistic feature and should be investigated in other languages.

(190) Speaker A. **buʔra**   **maala**   **ʔit-tooti**
  raw   meat   eat-2S.NEG.IMP
  'Don't eat a raw meat!'

  Speaker B. **buʔra**   *maa*   **ʔit-tooti**
  raw   what   eat-2S.NEG.IMP
  'Don't eat a raw what?'

5.2.6 Exclamatory Questions

These questions have a structure similar to Yes-No questions but have a force of an exclamatory assertion. Exclamatory questions are marked by a rising tone with a distinct surprise element.

(191) **kubb-inó!**
  jump-3MS.PPERF
  'He has jumped!' (I don't believe it!)

5.2.7 Direct and Indirect Questions

Sidaama distinguishes between direct and indirect questions.

5.2.7.1 Direct Questions

Direct questions are questions in which the interrogative clause is free and essentially have the same form to a content questions.

(192) **tewo**   **hiikka**   **haʔr-atto**
  today   where   go-2MS.IMPERF
  'Where will you go today?'

5.2.7.2 Indirect Questions

Indirect questions contain a dependent or subordinate interrogative structure. Such questions involve verbs, such as **t'a'm-** 'ask' in their matrix clause as shown below.

(193) **ʔise,** [**hiiko** **heeʔr-eemmo**   *gede*]   **t'aʔm-i-tú-ʔe**
  she   where   live-1MS.IMPERF   that   ask-EE-3FS.PERF-me
  'She asked me where I live?' (lit. 'She asked me where that I live?')

In (193) the structure inside the square brackets is an interrogative clause and it is subordinated by means of the complementiser **gede** 'that'. The sentence in (193) can be changed into a direct question as follows.

(194) **ʔise,**   ["**hiiko**   **heeʔr -aatto**"   **y-i-te**]   **t'aʔm-i-tú-ʔe**
    she   where live-2MS.IMPERF   say-EE-3FS.CVB   ask-EE-3FS.PERF-me
    'She asked me "where do you live?"'

The conversion of an indirect interrogative to a direct one gives rise to an interesting syntactic phenomenon. The interrogative clause requires an embedded form of **y-** 'verb to say' in order to support the interrogative clause.

5.2.8 Answers

Below we shall examine answers which are appropriate to each of the question types which were discussed earlier.

5.2.8.1 Answers to Content Questions

Answers to content questions can be full or abbreviated depending on the context and pragmatic conditions. Consider the interrogative sentence in (195) below with two types of answers: an abbreviated answer in (195b) and a full answer in (195c).

(195) a. Speaker A .   **min-i-ra**   *mamoote*   **haʔr-atto?**
             house-EE-to *when*   go-2MS.IMPERF
             'When will you go home?'

    b.   Speaker B .   **gaʔʔa**
                  'Tomorrow.'

    c.   Speaker B .   **gaʔʔa**   **haʔr-eemmo**
                  tomorrow go-1MS.IMPERF
                  'I shall go tomorrow'

Alternative questions which involve **–nso** 'or' have abbreviated answers with an inflected verb. The answer can be positive or negative depending on the question. For instance, if the alternative question contains the negative **di-** 'not', then the reply will also be in negative.

(196) Speaker A.   **loos-a-*nso***   **fooliššiʔr-a**   **hasiʔr-atto?**
             work-INF-or rest-INF   want-2MS.IMPERF
             'Do you like to rest or to work?'

    Speaker B.   **loos-a**   **hasiʔr-eemmo**

work-INF   want-1MS.IMPERF
'I want to work'

(197) Speaker A.   **ha?r-atto-*nso*   di-ha?r-atto?**
                      go-2MS.IMPERF-or   NEG-go-2MS.IMPERF
                      'Do you go or don't you?' (*lit.* 'Do you go or you don't go?')

        Speaker B.   **di-ha?r-eemmo**
                      NEG-go-1MS.IMPERF
                      'I shall not go'

5.2.8.2 Answers to Yes-No Questions

Replies to Yes-No questions can be single words of affirmation or negation, normally **ee** 'yes' or **dee'ni** 'no'.

(198) Speaker A.   **ga??a   k'a?e-ra   ha'r-atto-ní**
                      tomorrow home-to   go-2ms impf-Q
                      'Will you go home tomorrow?'

        Speaker B.   **?ee/dee?ni**   (abbreviated answer)
                      'Yes/No'

Replies to Yes-No questions, in addition to words of affirmation or negation, can include an inflected form of the interrogative verb.

(199) Speaker A.   **ga??a   k'a?e-ra   ha?r-atto-ní**
                      tomorrow home-to   go-2ms impf-Q
                      'Will you go home tomorrow?'

        Speaker B.   **?ee,   ha?r-eemmo**   (full answer)
                      'yes   go-1ms impf.
                      'Yes, I shall go'

Responses such as **hiitto gede** 'of course' and **dambe-te** 'certainly' represent a higher degree of affirmation for a Yes-No question as (180) below exemplifies.

(200) Speaker A.   **ga??a   k'a?e-ra   ha?r-atto-ní**
                      tomorrow home-to   go-2ms impf-Q.
                      'Will you go home tomorrow?'

        Speaker B.   **hiitto   gede**   (full affirmation)

how   like
'Certainly' (lit. 'And how!')

For a negative Yes-No question a positive answer can be provided. Note that although the answer word is positive the answer itself is negative. This is one of the interesting syntactic feature of Sidaama and which holds true also for Amharic and possibly other Ethiopian languages. This is exemplified under (201).

(201) Speaker A. **di-sirb-otto**
                    NEG-sing-2MS.PERF
                    'Didn't you sing?'

        Speaker B. **ʔee**
                    'Yes'

A response as in (201) can create ambiguity for speakers of other languages. However, if a word of affirmation is followed by a fully inflected verb the ambiguity can be avoided as exemplified below.

(202) Speaker A. **di-sirb-otto**
                    NEG-sing-2MS.PPERF
                    'Didn't you sing?'

        Speaker B. **ʔee,   di-sirb-ommo**
                    yes   NEG-sing-1MS.PPERF
                    'No, I didn't sing.' (*lit.* 'Yes, I didn't sing').

5. 3 Modals

Modals subsume imperatives and jussives. Imperatives are differentiated from other clause types in that they require 2nd persons only as their subject as exemplified under (203).

(203) a. **min-i-ra   haʔr-i**[33]
            house-EE-to   go-2SG.IMP
            Go home!' (sg.)

---

[33] As indicated in the morphology section, stress has a grammatical function in Sidaama. The 2nd sg. imperative is indicated by /i/ while the 3rd ms. pf. is marked by /í/, i.e. a stressed vowel. Contrast the following two examples.
a. **haʔr–i**   'go!' (2sg.)   b. **haʔr–i**   'He went'.
     go–2MS.IMP   go–3MS.PERF

b. **min-i-ra**   **hadʼ-ɗe**[34]
home-EE-to   go-2PL.IMP
'Go home!' (pl.)

In (203) the subject is a 2nd masculine singular although it is not overt. This can be proved by adding **koo** a 2nd masculine singular vocative pronoun to the imperative in (204).

(204) **koo,**   **min-i-ra**   **haʔr-i**
you   home-EE-to   go-2SG.IMP
'You, go home!'

There is a semantic differences between the imperatives in (203) and (204). The former is a normal command while the latter is a command which also carries a tone of warning.

The other structure which belongs to the category of modals is the jussive. A jussive is a mild form of imperative and as such is restricted to 1st and 3rd persons only. Consider the examples below.

(205) a. **daafurs-i,**   **min-i-ra**   **haʔr-ona**
Daafursa-NOM   home-EE-to   go-3MS.JUSS
'Let Daafursa go home.'

b. **ʔan-i**   **dikko**   **haʔr-ona**
I-NOM   market   go-1SG.JUSS
'Let me go to the market.'

5.4 Complex Sentences

Complex sentences, in their narrower sense, are sentences which consist of one matrix clause and one or more subordinate clauses. In their broader sense, complex sentences also include compound sentences which comprise two or more matrix clauses. There are two types of subordinate clauses in Sidaama:. non-embedded and embedded.

5.4.1 Non-Embedded Subordinate clauses

Non-embedded clauses do not substitute for the phrases in a simple clause. Such clauses are

---

[34] The hypothetical 2nd pl. imperative formative is */–te/. If a verb ends in a single consonant, that consonant will be geminated by assimilating into the suffix–initial /t/. However, if a verb stem ends in a geminate or cluster, the suffix–initial /t/ will be elided.

introduced in Sidaama by a subordinating conjunctions: **-ro** 'if', **daafira** 'because', **nafunni** 'even if', etc. Consider the examples under (206).

(206) a. [**woʔmanka wote dod-i-*ro***],   k'olčanšo   k'eel-anno]
       all   time   run-3MS.PERF-if   race   win-3MS.IMPERF
       'If he runs always, he will win the race.'

    b. [**fatana   saʔ-inó**   *daafira*],   **ʔegenn-aammo   ʔikk-í**]
       exam   pass-3MS.PPERF   because   know-NMZ   become-3MS.PERF
       'He became famous because he has passed the exam.'

    c. [**dod-itto-ro**   *nafunni*],   **min-i-ra**   **di-ʔiill-atto**]
       run-2MS.PERF-if   even if   home-EE-to   NEG-reach-2MS.IMPERF
       'Even if you run, you will not reach home.'

5.4.2 Embedded Subordinate Clauses

There are three types of embedded clauses in Sidaama: complement clauses, relative clauses and subjectless sentences.

5.4.2.1 Complement Clauses

A complement clause substitutes for an entire NP as a subject or object and is introduced by **complementizers**. Sidaama has two types of complements. the **-ra** 'to' and **gede** 'that' complement.

(i) The -*ra* Complement

The **-ra** complement is formed by suffixing **-ra** to an imperfective verb.

(207) a. [**min-i-ra**   **haʔr-eemmo-*ra***]   **hasi'r-eemmo**
       home-EE-to   go-1MS.IMPERF-to   want-1MS.IMPERF
       'I want to go home.'

    b. **beša,** [**Don-i**   **min-i-ra**   **haʔr- inó**]   *gede]*   **ʔaf-finó**
       Besha Dona-NOM home-EE-to   go-3MS.PPERF that   know-3FS.PPERF
       'Besha knows that Dona has gone home.'

One of the syntactic characteristics of the **-ra** complement clause is its selection of coreferential subjects in the complement clause and the matrix clause as shown in (208).

(208) a. [**(ʔan-i),**   [**waa   ʔag-eemmo-ra**]   **hasʔir-eemo**]

(I-NOM) water drink-1MS.IMPERF-to want-1MS.IMPERF
'I want to drink water.'

b. [sarmiso, [waa ?ag-a-ra][35] has?ir-anno]
Sarmiso water drink-3MS.IMPERF-to want-3MS.IMPERF
'Sarmiso wants to drink water.'

In (208) above the subject of the matrix clause and that of the embedded clause are coreferential. For instance in (208a) this can be deduced from the shape of the inflectional suffix -eemmo which is a 1MS.IMPERF. Syntactically the -ra complement functions as an object complement for the verb of the matrix clause. For instance in (208a) the complement clause [waa ?ag-eemmo-ra] 'to drink water' functions as an object for the matrix verb hasi?r- 'want'.

The other syntactic characteristic of the -ra complement is that, when it is stripped of its complementizer -ra, it has the same form as a sentence-like (S-like) complement. According to Bresnan (1985: 49) a sentence-like complement is "one that without complementizers has roughly the same syntactic form as a main clause". For instance the S-like complement of (208a) would be as follows.

(209) [[waa ?ag-eemmo]
water drink-1MS.IMPERF
'I shall drink water.'

(ii) The -gede Complement

This complement is formed by suffixing the -gede 'that' to an embedded verb. Sentence (210) exemplifies this.

(210) [[Turbo k'olč-anšo k'eel-anno gede] ?af-oommo]
Turbo take over-NMZ win-3MS.IMPERF that know-1MS.IMPERF
'I know that Turbo will win the race.'

The gede complement functions as a subject complement of *impersonal passives* or as an object complement of *epistemic* or *desiderative* predicates. Consider the example below.

(211) a. [[?ayaan-u ga??a hos-anno gede] ?egenn-i-noonni]
holiday-NOM tomorrow occur-3MS.IMPERF that know-EE-IMPRS.PASS
'It is known that the holiday will take place tomorrow.'

---

[35] Note that when -ra is attached to the imperfect of 3rd persons the **nno** part of the suffix is deleted.

b. [[**manč-u** **ga??a** **da-anno** *gede*] **?af-oommo**]
    man-NOM   tomorrow come-3MS.IMPERF that   know-1MS.PPERF
    'I know that the man will come tomorrow.'

In (211a) the *gede* complement functions as a subject complement for the impersonal passive
?egenn-i-noonni 'it is known'. This verb is marked as impersonal by virtue of taking the
impersonal subject marker –**noonni**. In (211b) the *gede* complement functions as an object of
the epistemic verb **?af-** 'know'.

The *gede* complement allows either coreferential NPs (as in 212a) or non-coreferential NPs
(as in 212b) in the complement clause and in the matrix clause.

(212) a. [[**k'olčanšo** **k'eel-eemmo** *gede*] **?af-oommo**]
      race   win-1MS.IMPERF that   know-1MS.PPERF
      'I know that I shall win the race.'

    b. [[**k'olčanšo** **k'eel-anno** *gede*] **?af-oommo**]
      race   win-3MS.IMPERF that   know-1MS.PPERF
      'I know that he will win the race.'

Regarding tense/aspect choice, the –**gede** complement has no constraint on the complement
clause. On the other hand the tense/aspect of the matrix can be perfect or present perfect but
not imperfect.

5.4.2.2 Relative Clauses

Relative clauses are clauses which modify head nouns in NPs. Consider (213) in which the
relative clauses are italicised.

(213) a. [[**bero** *day-inó*] **beett-i**], **maat'-am-í**
      yesterday come-3MS.PPERF boy-NOM   hide-PASS-3MS.PERF
      'The boy who came yesterday hid himself.'

    b. [[**bero** *haɗ-dinó*] **mannooti**], **tewo** **hig-ganno**
      yesterday go-3PL.PPERF men   today   return-3PL.IMPERF
      'The men who went yesterday will return today.'

Altough the above sentences are relatives, the suffixes which mark them are absent. This is
because the clauses contain a head noun. If a head noun of a relative is deleted, then the suffix
which marks it will be realized overtly as shown below.

(214) a. [[**bero**   *day-inó-h-u*]   **maat'-am-í**
       yesterday   come-3MS.PPERF-REL.M-NOM   hide-PASS-3MS.PERF
       'The one who came yesterday hid himself.'

Relative clauses in Sidaama fall into two classes: restrictive and non-restrictive (appositive). From the semantic point of view, a restrictive relative clause specifies the class of entities referred to by the head noun as shown under (215).

(215) [[**bero**   [**ʔado   ʔag-inó**   **beett-i**]],   **ʔane-wa   day-í**]
       yesterday   milk   drink-3MS.PPERF   boy-NOM   me-to   come-3MS.PERF
       'The boy who drank the milk yesterday came to me.'

In sentence (215) the structure before the word **beett-i** 'the boy' is a restrictive relative clause. It is restrictive in the sense that the structure [[**ʔado ʔag-inó**] 'who drank milk' specifies what the head noun **beetto** 'the boy' has performed. A restrictive relative clause is also distinguished phonologically in that it is separated from the matrix clause by means of a single intonation boundary as shown in example (215). A non-restrictive relative clause adds additional, albeit extraneous, information about the head noun. Consider the example below.

(216) [**Hawaasa   heeʔr-anno,**   *jaal-i-'ya*],   **bero**   **day-í**
       Hawaasa   live-REL-NOM   friend-NOM-my   yesterday   come-3MS.PERF
       'My friend, who lives in Hawaasa, came yesterday.'

In the above example the relative [**Hawaasa   heeʔr-anno**] 'one who lives in Hawaasa' is non-restrictive because this information is incidental and not crucial for the head noun [**jaal-i-'ya**] 'my friend'.

5.4.2.3 Subjectless Sentences

All sentence types which were discussed until now have subject NPs. Pronominal NP subjects are typically absent because their information content is present in the pronominal suffixes attached to the verb. In some sentences the subject is not realized overtly. Nevertheless, its status can be deduced from various suffixes found attached to the verb. Such sentences which do not have a phonetically realized subject are known as *subjectless* sentences. The types of verbs associated with subjectless sentences are also restricted. These are *eventive, existential,* and *passive* verbs and each verb type has a corresponding sentence type.

Eventive sentences contain head verbs such as **ʔikk-** 'become', **lab-** 'appear/seem' and copulatives such as **-ti** 'is' which could function as a main verb of an eventive clause as exemplified below.

(217) [[**beett-u,   min-i-ra   haʔr-inó-ha**]   **law-anno**]

boy-NOM house-EE-to   go-3MS.PPERF-REL   appear-3MS.IMPERF
'It seems that the boy went home.'

The second group of eventive sentences is based on the copulative verb -**ti** 'is'. It differs from the first group of eventive verbs such as -**lab**- 'seem' because they do not require a relativizer.

(218) [[**guyye**   **hando**   **hidɗ-a-si**]-**ti**]
       Guyye   ox   buy-INF-his-is
       'Guyye is buying (is going to buy) an ox.'

In the above example the whole embedded structure [**guyye** **hando hidɗ -a-si**] 'Guyye's buying of an ox' is an infinitive phrase which together with the copula –**ti** 'is' forms the complex sentence.

Existential clauses are based on **no**- which is a 'verb of presence'. If object pronominal suffixes are attached to this verb it indicates possession. Consider (219) below.

(219) a. **sarmiso,**   **gobba**   **no**
       Sarmiso   outside   present (3MS)
       'Sarmiso is outside.'

     b. **sarmiso-ra,**   **min-u**   **noo-si**
       Sarmiso-for   house-NOM   has-him
       'Sarmiso has a house.' (*lit.* 'For Sarmiso there is a house')
Sidaama existential clauses, unlike similar verbs, do not have complex forms.

A passive sentence contains a passive subject and its verb is marked by the suffix –**am**. Consider the following simple passive sentence.

(220) [**daafurs-i,**   **k'eel-am-i**]
       Daafursa-NOM   defeat-PASS-3MS.PERF
       'Daafursa was defeated.'

In the above sentence the passive verb **k'eel-am** 'was defeated' has an active counterpart **k'eel**- 'win'.

5.4.2.4 Complex Interrogative Sentences

Sentence (221b) is a simple interrogative counterpart of sentence (221a).

(221) (a) [*daafurs*-**i,**   **waa**   **ʔag-í**]

who-NOM   Water   drink-3MS.PERF
'Daafursa drank water.'

(b) [*ay*-**i**,   **waa**   **ʔag-í**
      who-NOM water   drink-3MS.PERF
      'Who drank water?'

The question can be made more complex by making use of relative clauses. For instance one can question the subject of the above sentence.

(222) [[**waa**   **ʔag-inó-h-u**]   *ʔayee*-**ti**]
      water   drink-3MS.PPERF-REL.M-NOM who-is
      'Who is it that has drunk water?'

What we have observed above is a questioning of the subject. Likewise it is possible to question the direct object [**waa**] 'water' of sentence (201a). Thus, the simple question version of it will be as in (203a) and its complex version as in (203b).

(223) a. [**daafurs-i**,   *maa*   **ʔag-í**]
        Daafursa-NOM what   drink-3MS.PERF
        'What did Daafursa drink?'

      b. [**daafurs-i**,   **ʔag-inó-h-u**   *maa-ti*]
        Daafursa-nom.   drink-3MS.PPERF-REL.M-NOM *what*-is
        'What is that Daafursa has drunk?'

Although the above order is the default one, it is possible to move the interrogative clause to another position as in (c).

      c. *maa-ti*   [**daafurs-i**   **ʔag-inó-h-u**]
        what-is   Daafursa-NOM drink-3MS.PPERF-REL.M-NOM
        'What is it that Daafursa has drunk?'

In (223c) [*maa-ti*] 'what is?' was moved from a VP position and is placed outside the sentence. The only position available outside the sentence is topic position. Hence [*maa-ti*] 'what is is?' is moved to topic position: the highest position in any clausal structure where a grammatical element attains more prominence than other constituents.

The structure [*maa-ti*] can be moved to a sentence-medial position as in (224).

(224) [[**daafurs-i**   *maa-ti*]   **ʔag-inó-h-u**]

Daafursa-NOM   what-is   drink-3MS.PPERF-REL.M-NOM
'What is that Daafursa has drunk?'

Complex interrogative clauses can question either the subject or the object. One can also pose various types of adverbial questions. For instance one of this is known as a causal interrogative.

(225) [**daafurs-i**   **t'ook'-inó-h-u,**   *maaye-ra*-**ti**]?
Daafursa-nom.   flee-3MS.PPERF-REL.M-NOM   what-for-is
'Why did Daafursa flee?' (*lit.* 'It is for what that Daafursa fled?')

5.4.2.5 Cleft Sentences

Cleft sentences are formed by relativizing the verb of the simple sentence and by suffixing a copula to the focussed constituent. Consider the simple sentences in (226) and their cleft counterparts in (226).

(226) a. [**ʔat-i**   [**daafursa**   **kaaʔl-ootto**]]
you-NOM   Daafursa   help-2MS.PPERF
'You have helped Daafursa.'

b. [**ʔan-i**   [**ʔado**   **ʔag-oommo**]]
I-nom.   milk   drink-1MS.PPERF
'I have drunk milk.'

(227) a. [[**daafursa**   **kaaʔl-ootto-h-u**],   **ʔatee-ti**]
Daafursa   help-2MS.PPERF-REL.M-NOM   you-is
'The one who has helped Daafursa is you.'

b. [[**ʔado**   **ʔag-oommo-h-u**]],   **ʔanee-ti**]
milk   drink-1ms ppf-rel(m.)-nom.   me-is
'The one who has drunk the milk is me.'

The structures in (227) are not the only possibilities for showing emphasis. For instance it is possible to extrapose the VP to a topic, i.e. a pre-sentence position. Thus, sentences (226a) and (b) can have the following structure.

(228) a. [*ʔatee-ti*,   [**daafursa**   **kaaʔl-ootto-h-u**]]
you-is   Daafursa   help-2MS.PPERF-REL.M-NOM
'It is you who have helped Daafursa.'

b. [*ʔanee-ti*, [ʔado ʔag-oommo-h-u]]
    me-is   milk   drink-1MS.PPERF-REL.M-NOM
    'It is I who have drunk milk.'

The comma which is placed after the topic sentences of (228) represents a pause. A pause, as was mentioned previously, is one of the illocutionary strategies employed by Sidaama speakers for the purpose of getting prominence or attention.

It is not only a subject which can be focussed. Sidaama allows the focussing of a direct object, an indirect (dative) object, an adverb and a PP. First let us consider a simple sentence in (229) and then the focussing of a direct object and an indirect object in (229a and b), respectively.

(229) a. [waayyiso [beetto-te uddano ʔuy-inó]]
          Waayyiso   girl-to   cloth   give-3MS.PERF
          'Waayyiso has given a cloth to the girl.'

      b. [[beetto-te-ti] waayyiso ʔuddano ʔuy-inó-h-u]]
          girl-to-is   Waayyiso cloth   give-3MS.PPERF-REL.M-NOM
          'It is to the girl that Waayyiso has given a cloth.'

      c. [[ʔuddano-te] waayyiso beetto-te ʔuy-inó-h-u]]
          cloth-is   Waayyiso girl-to   give-3MS.PPERF-REL.M-NOM
          'It is a cloth that Waayyiso has given to the girl.

The other constituents which could be focussed are adverbs and PPs. Consider the cleft sentences in (230).

(230) a. [[sikk'o-te-nni-ti]   [waayyiso hando gan-inó-h-u]]
          stick-GEN.F-with-is   Waayyiso   ox   beat-3MS.PPERF-REL.M-NOM
          'It is with a stick that Waayyiso has beaten the ox.'

      b. [[bero-ti   [waayyiso min-i-ra   haʔr-inó-h-u]]
          yesterday   Waayyiso   home-EE-to go-3MS.PPERF-REL.M-NOM
          'It is yesterday that Waayyiso has gone home.'

5.5 Compound Sentences

These are sentences in which two coordinate clauses are conjoined by the suffix **-nna** 'and' or the word **woy** 'or'. Sidaama allows **-nna** conjunctions within a simple sentence as illustrated below.

(231) a. [harimo   hando-nna   gaango   hidd-í]

Harimo   ox-and   mule   buy-3MS.PERF
'Haarimo bought an ox and a mule.'

b. [**harimo**   **faraššo,**   **hando-nna**   **gaango**   **hidd-í**]
   Harimo   horse   ox-and   mule   buy-3MS.PERF
   'Harimo bought a horse, an ox and a mule.'

Sidaama dos not allow two sentences to be conjoined by -**nna** 'and'. On the other hand, compounds which are conjoined by **woy** 'or' are allowed. Consider the following sentence.

(232) [**waa**   **ʔag-i**   *woy*   **ʔado**   **ʔag-i**]
       water   drink-2SG.IMP   or   milk   drink-2SG.IMP
       'Drink water or drink milk!'

There is another possibility for conjoining the above two clauses. This involves insertion of the coordinator **woy** 'or' at the beginning of each clause. Consider (233) which is repeated below.

(233) [*woy* **waa**   **ʔag-i**   *woy*   **ʔado**   **ʔag-i**]
       or   water   drink-2SG.IMP   or   milk   2SG.IMP
       'Either drink water or either drink milk!'

5.6 Adverbial Clauses

Adverbials have various functions in the grammatical structure of Sidaama. They can modify a clause from the point of view of time, manner, place, purpose, etc. Accordingly, five adverbial clause types are distinguished. These are: Conditional, Concessive, Temporal, Purposive, Counterfactual and Reason clauses. Aspect and various grammatical elements play a role in the distinction of the adverbials.

5.6.1 Conditional Clauses

Two type of conditional clause are identified in Sidaama: reality/possible conditional (realis) and hypothetical//improbable conditional (irrealis). In reality conditionals the subordinate clause contains the 'if-clause' (protasis) and this is followed by the main clause (apodosis). The protasis is marked by -**ro** 'if' which is always suffixed to a verb in perfective aspect while the apodosis always contains a verb which is inflected in the imperfective aspect or in the imperative.

(234) (a) **ros-i-tto-ro,**   **fatana**   **saʔ-atto**
           learn-EE-PERF-CND   exam   pass-2SG.M.IMPERF
           'If you study you will pass the exam.'

    (b)   **daafur-i-tto-ro,**   **buna**   **ʔag-i**
          become tire-EE-PERF-CND   coffee   drink-2SG.IMP
          'If you are tired drink coffee!'

In hypothetical conditional the the protasis is marked by **-ro** 'if' which is suffixed to a verb in present perfect while the apodosis contains a verb in imperfective to which the preventive **-nka** 'would have' is suffixed as shown below.

(235) a. **ros-ootto-ro,**   **fatana**   **saʔ-atto-nka**
          learn-2SG.M.PPERF-CND exam   pass-2SG.M.IMPERF-would have
          'Had you studied , you would have passed the exam.'

5.6.2 Concessive Clauses

In concessives of Sidaama the protasis contains **nafuu ~ nafunni** 'even if' and the verb **ikk-** 'be/become'. Regarding the aspectual structure, concessives are similar to reality conditionals. The difference between the two is positive vs. negative marking. Accordingly, if the protasis is positive the apodosis will be in negative (or a verb which marks "failures") and vice versa. Negation of protasis is marked by **hoog-** 'unable' to which the conditional marker**-ro** is attached.

(236) (a) **worba**   **nafuu**   **ikk-i-ro,**   **tunso**   **waaj-janno**
          brave   even if   be-EE-CND darkness fear-2SG.M.IMPERF
          'Even if he is brave, he is fearful of darkness.'

    (b) **worba** **nafuu** **ikk-a** **hoog-i-ro,**   **tunso**   **di-waaj-janno**
          brave   even if be-INF unable-PERF-CND darkness NEG-fear-3SG.M.IMPERF
          'Even if he is not brave, he is not fearful of darkness.'

5.6.3 Tempoal Clauses

Sidaama distinguishes two types of temporal clauses: sequential and simultaneous. In sequential clauses, the subordinate clause is marked by **-wote** 'when, at the time' which is juxtaposed to the main verb. In addition, in sequential clauses both the subordinate and main clauses can take all the three aspects.

(237) (a) **yon-i**   **gooʔr-í**   **wote,**   **waa**   **ʔag-í**
          Yona-NOM thirsty-3SG.M.PERF when   water drink-3MS.PERF
          'When Yona became thirsty he drank water.'

(b) **yon-i**   **go?r-anno**   **wote,**   **waa**   **?ag-anno**
      Yona-NOM   thirsty-3SG.M.IMPERf   when   water   drink-3MS.IMPERF
      'When Yona becomes thirsty he drinks water.'

Simultaneity is marked by the 'continuous marker' **-anni** when the subject of the matrix and subordinate clause are co-referential.

(238) **beett-u**   **fiik'-anni**   **dod-anno**
        boy-NOM   whistle-CONT   run-3SG.M.IMPERF
        'The boy runs while whistling.'

The main clause allows all the three aspects. Hence the main verb of the above example can be substituted either by **dod-ino** 'he has run' or **dod-í** 'he ran'. If the subject of the matrix and subordinate clause are not co-referential, then **-anna** marks simultaneity. Furthermore, the subordinate clause can take all the three aspects.

(239) **yon-i**   **sirb-anna**   **beša**   **šaye**   **ag-anno**
        Yona-NOM   sing-CONT   Besha   tea   drink-3MS.IMPERF
        'While Yona sings Besha drinks tea.'

In (239) the verb of the main clause can be either in perfect as in **ag-gú** 'she drank' or in present perfect as in **ag-gino** 'she has drank'.

5.6.4 Purposive Clauses

A purposive clause carries the meaning 'in order to' or 'so that'. In such clauses, the subordinate clause is marked either by the complementizer **gede** 'in order that' or by the subordinator **-ra** 'to'. In purposive clauses, the subordinate clause is always in imperfective while the matrix clause can take different aspects as shown below.

(240) **?uddano**   **?abb-anno**   **gede,**   **rodoo-si**   **soy-í**
        cloth   bring-3MS.IMPERF   COMP   brother-his   send-3MS.PERF
        'He sent his brother in order to bring clothes.'

In sentence (240) the main verb **soy-í** 'he sent' can also be replaced by **soy-ino** 'he has sent' or **soy-anno** 'he will send'. If the subject of the matrix and dependent clause are co-referential then the purposive will have a different structure. The verb of the subordinate clause will be infinitival to which the dative **-te** is suffixed. The aspect of the main verb has no restriction. It can be perfect, present perfect or imperfect.

(241) **beeto**   **buna**   **gaf-a-te,**   **giira**   **giir-tú**

girl   coffee   boil-to-DAT   fire   burn-3FS.PERF COMP
'The girl burned the fire in order to boil coffee.'

In the above sentence the infinitival **gaf-a-te** 'in order to boil' can be optionally followed by the converb of the quotative verb **y-** 'say' without change in meaning as illustrated below.

(242) **beeto   buna   gaf-a-te,   y-i-te,   giira giir-tú**
       girl   coffee   boil-to-DAT say-EE-3FS.CNV fire burn-3FS.PERF
       'The girl burned the fire in order to boil coffee.'

5.6.5 Counterfactuals

The subordinate in counterfactuals (preventive) is always in present perfect while the main clause is can be either in imperfect or present perfect which is followed by the preventive suffix **-nka**.

(243) **wot'e   afiʔr-oommo-ro   makiina hidʄ-oommo-nka**
       money   get-1MS.PPERF-CND   car   buy-1MS.PPERF-PRVN
       'If I got a money, I would have bought a car.'

5.6.6 Reason Clauses

In reason clauses the subordinate clause is either in imperfect or present perfect while the aspect of the main clause can be in all of the three aspects. The verb of the subordinate clause is followed by the relative **-hu** to which the dative **–ra** 'to' is suffixed.

(244) **wot'e   ʔuy-ino-ʔe-hu-ra   galat-ummo-si**
       money   give-3MS.PPERF-me-REL-because thank-1MS.PERF-him
       'I thanked him because he gave me money.'

A reason clause can be periphrastically expressed by suffixing **daafira** 'because' to the subordinate verb instead of sequentially suffixing the relative **-hu** to and the dative **–ra**.

(245) **wajj-anno   daafira   fatana   di-saʔ-ino**
       afraid-3MS.IMPERF   because   exam   NEG-pass-3MS.PPERF
       'Because he is fearful he didn't pass the exam.'

6. Ideophones and Interjections

Dingemanse (2011a: 25) defines an ideophone as "words that depict sensory imagery" in order to handle broader ranges available in various languages. Sidaama ideophones have phonological, morphological and syntactic peculiarities. Nevertheless they are similar to other word classes in that they can undergo inflection or derivation.

6.1 Predicative Ideophones

Most of the ideophones in Sidaama are predicative ideophones which co-occur with the "qouatative" verb **y-** 'say' or **ʔass-** 'do'. Those verbs which occur with **y-** 'say' are intransitive while those which take **ʔass-** are transitive. The example below and others are based on the infinitive suffix **-a**.

(246)   **hikk'i y-í** 'He hiccupped.'   **hikk'i ʔass-í**   'He caused somebody to hiccup.'

The first part of the ideophones are usually fixed and hardly undergo morphological processes. It is the second part i.e. the verbal part to which inflectional suffixes can be attached. Here is a list of some of predicative ideophones which have both intransitive and transitive forms. The intransitive ideophones are on left handside while the transitive ones are on the right.

(247) i.   **šikk'i**   **y-a** 'to approach'   **šikk'i**   **ʔass-a** 'to bring near'
    ii.   **milli**   **y-a** 'to move' (INTR)   **milli**   **ʔass-a** 'to move' (TR)
    iii.   **k'upp'i**   **y-a** 'to squat'   **k'upp'i**   **ʔass-a** 'cause to squat'

6.2 Ideophones and Phonetic Symbolism

One of the phonological features which characterizes Sidaama ideophones is the occurrence of nasal vowels accompanied with a geminate **ʔ/h** or the presence of a nasal without a geminate **ʔ/h**. This combination never occurs in other words. These ideophones are usually associated with movement of a mouth or with different sounds emitted by humans/animals and are listed below.

(248) a.   **ʔãʔʔã**   **y-a**   'to groan' (because of pain)
    b.   **hãhhã**   **y-a**   'to open mouth wide'   (INTR)
    c.   **hũʔʔũ**   **y-a**   'to bellow' (sound made by oxen)
    d.   **hiññi**   **y-a**   'to bare the teeth'
    e.   **ñammi**   **ʔass-a** 'to taste'

Ideophones with the high vowels /i/ and /u/ are associated with light emission and fast movements as exemplified below.

(249)	a.	**biličč'i**	**y-a**	'to be resplendent, to light on'
	b.	**dirgimmi**	**y-a**	'to disappear all of a sudden, to light off'
	c.	**furduggi**	**y-a**	'to pop out suddenly'
	d.	**lipp'i**	**ʔass-a**	'to twinkle the eyes'
	d.	**k'ipp'i**	**ʔass-a**	'to wink at'

6.3 Ideophones and Derivation

One of the major derivational process observed in ideophones is the changing of intransitive verbs into transitive ones. Since the first part of the ideophone is usually fixed, this is achieved by changing the second part of the ideophone i.e. the verb. During such process, the intransitive y- 'say' is substituted by the transitive **ass-** 'do'. The relevant examples appear under (248) and (249) and will not be repeated here.

Despite of this restriction, a number of ideophones allow derivation by allowing a change in their first part of the compound. In such cases, the output is a noun.

(250)	a.	**hawwu**	**y-a**	'to be dizzy'	**hawwu-naate**	'dizziness'
	b.	**lipp'i**	**ʔass-a**	'to twinkle the eyes'	**lipp'-o**	'twinkling of the eye'

A pair of ideophones allow coordination. In such ideophones the constituent parts carry opposite meanings.

(251) a. **biličč'i-nna dirgimmi y-a** 'to light on and off'
   (**biličč'i y-a** 'to light on' **dirgimmi y-a** 'to light off')

   b. **hobbi-nna rutt'i   y-a** 'to hesitate'
   (**hobbi y-a** 'to brandish a spear' **rutt'i   y-a** 'to withdraw')

6.4 Interjections

An interjection is a word that is used to express a sentiment or an emotion on the part of the speaker. Interjections differ from ideophones in that they do not undergo morphological processes or enter into syntactic relationships. Hence interjections are unproductive and form a closed class. According to Ameka (1992, 1994) interjections can be classified into three groups: 'expressive', 'conative' and 'phatic' interjections.

6.4.1 Expressive Interjections

They express the speaker's emotions and most Sidaama interjections belong to this class.

(252) a. **haššu** 'exclamation of happiness' (mostly on hearing positive news)[36]
 b. **hay hay** 'alas!, exclamation of sorrow'
 c. **hoola** 'exclamation of surprise, my goodness!'
 d. **ʔunša** 'woe to!' (sorrow for the bad lack that falls on somebody)
 e. **baysibaʔo** 'exclamation of sorrow, alas!'[37]
 f. **ʔaanneʔye** 'exclamation of sorrow, alas!' (on death of somebody)

6.4.2 Conative Interjections

This class contains various sorts of interjections. It includes responses to calls, invitations and animal calls. The response to a call made by a male or female speaker is **yee** 'yes'. The call can be made by using a proper noun, the father/mother of X for instance **guyye ʔanna/ʔama** 'Guyye's father/mother' or teknonymy as in **ʔabba guyye** 'Guyye's father'. If one offers something to somebody, he will utter **hīīʔi** 'take!' (SG) and **hīīʔʔe**'take!' (PL). Among animal calls, the prevalent one is **lukku lukku** a call made to chicken.

6.4.3 Phatic Interjections

It contains sounds made while listening to somebody's speech. The pair of words **ʔee** and **ʔeeyya** are used to signal that one is paying attention to a speech of another and urges him to continue. On the other hand, when one listens a folktale he uses the expression **ʔeeyyatʼa** after every sentence to signal that he is following the tale.

---

[36] It can also be used when a kid hurts himself despite the warning of his parents or siblings and is uttered to say 'you got what you deserve'.

[36] The expression **baysibaʔo** is derived from:

baʔ–e	is–i	baʔ–o
be loose–3MS.CNV	he–NOM	loose–3MS.PPERF

'Being lost let him be lost'

Sample Texts

In this section two sample texts are presented. The first text is entitled "**k'uč'-u-nna hilleess-u k'olčanšo**". It is a translation of Aesop's Fable "The Tortoise and the Hare" from Amharic into Sidaama. It is selected to show how Sidaama copes with stories translated from another language. The second text is a native Sidaama tale entitled "**doobbiičč-u bank'o aɗɗ-a has?ir-ino**". It can be roughly translated as "The Lion Wanted to Marry a Thunder". For ease of presentation and analysis, the text is segmented into individual sentences. Each sentence is presented with an inter-linear morphemic labelling. This is followed by a free translation of the sentence. Extrapolated meaning is enclosed within square brackets. In addition, some linguistic remarks are included in the footnotes to clarify some special structures or lexical collocations of Sidaama.

Text 1 k'uč'-u-nna hilleess-u k'olč-anšo "The Race between the Tortoise and the Hare"

k'uč'-u-nna	hilleess-u	k'olč-anšo
tortoise-NOM-and	hare-NOM	race-NMNLZR

'The race Between the Tortoise and the Hare'

1.

mitto	barra	k'uč'-u-nna	hilleess-u	doogo-teɪ	?iima
one	day	tortoise-NOM-and	hare-NOM	road-by	upon

t'aad-dú
meet-3PL.PERF

'One day a tortoise and a hare met [each other] on the road.'

2.

hilleess-u-no	k'uč'a,	"koo	dunka	hiikkira	ha?r-atto?"
Hare-NOM-and	tortoise	you	slow	where	go-2M.SG.IMPERF

y-ii-si
say-3MS.PERF-him

'The hare said to the tortoise "you sluggish, where are you going?" '

3.

k'uč'-u-no	?aaram-e,		"maayra	dunka
tortoise-NOM-and	enraged-3MS.CONV		why	sluggish

y-aatto-?e?		hasi?r-itto-ro,	?amo	k'olč-am-mo"
say-2M.SG-IMPERF-1SG.OBJ		want-2M.SG-PPERF-if	come!	race-PASS-1PL.JUSS

y-ii-si
say-3MS.PERF-him

'The tortoise being enraged said to him [to the hare], "if you want, come! let us compete in a race.'

4. **k'uč'-u-no**   **"maayye"**   **y-í**
   tortoise-NOM-and   okay   say-3MS.PERF
   'And the tortoise said to him [to the hare] "okay". '

5. **k'olčansho-te₂**   **darga**   **marat'-t'ú**   **gedensaanni,**   **yeedal-čo**
   race-of   place   choose-3PL.PERF   after   fox-SGV

   daañña   **ʔass-i-tú-se**
   judge   make-EE-3PL-her
   'After choosing the place of the race, they made a vixen a judge.'

6. **yeedal-čo-no**   **"mite,**   **lame,**   **sase!"**   **y-i-te₃-nna**   **k'olč-ansho**
   fox-SGV-and   one,   two   three   say-EE-3FS.CONV-and   race-NMZ

   jamar-an-tú
   begin-PASS-3FS.PERF
   'The vixen said [counted] one, two, three and the race began.'

7. **hilleess-u-no**   **k'uč'a**   **hakka**   **woonte-nni³⁸**   **k'olč-í-si**
   hare-NOM-and   tortoise   there   time-POST   outrace-3MS.PERF-3
   'And the hare outraced the tortoise *immediately* [*lit.* there and then].'

8. **k'uč'-u**   **kayni**   **lowo geessha**   **baɗɗ-i-ra**   **gat-í**
   tortoise-NOM   but   very much   back-EE-to   remain-3MS.PERF
   'However, the tortoise remained very much rearwards.'

9. **hilleess-u-no**   **k'uč'a**   **ʔagar-a-ra**   **y-e³⁹**   **haaysso-te₁**
   hare-NOM-and   tortoise   wait-INF-to   say-3MS.CONV   grass-GEN.F

   ʔiima   **dolli**   **y-í**
   on   doze   say-3MS.PERF
   'The hare dozed off on top of the grass in order to wait for the tortoise.'

10. **hakka**   **wote-no**   **got'-ano**   **ʔaɗɗ-i-tú-si**
    there   time-and   sleep-NMZ   take-EE-3FS.PERF-him
    'And at that moment he slept [*lit.* sleep took him].'

11. **k'uč'-u-no**   **sunuu-nni**   **haʔr-anni**   **k'olčanšo-te**
    hare-NOM-and   slow-with   go-3MS.CONT   race-of

---

³⁸ The expression **hakka woontenni** 'immediately' has a variant **hakka woteni**.

³⁹ The structure infinitive + **-ra** followed by the converb of the verb **y-** 'say' can be interpreted as "in order to V", where V represents the infinitival form of verb.

mač'č'araš-i   darga   ʔill-í
end-of   place   reach-3MS.PERF
'And the tortoise walking slowly reached to the final point of the race.'

12.   hilleess-u-no   laʔ-asine   k'uč'a-ho   č'awač'č'abb-anna
     hare-NOM-and   look-PL.NMZ   tortoise-to   clap hands-CONT

     mač'č'iišš-e   got'ano-tenni   kaʔ-í
     hear-3MS.CONV   sleep-from   wake up-3MS.PERF
     'And the hare woke up from his sleep upon hearing the spectators clapping
     [their] hands for the tortoise.'

13.   lowo geešša-no   ʔaaram-í
     very much-and   enraged-3MS.PERF
     'And he was enraged very much.'

14.   k'eel-am-ino-ta-no   ʔaf-e,   k'uč'a
     Win-PASS-3MS.PPERF-REL-and   realize-3MS.PERF   tortoise

     "laaynki-meeššo   di-t'on-eemmo-he"   y-ii-si
     second-time   NEG-curse-1MS.IMPERF-you   say-3MS.PERF-him
     'And he knew that he was defeated and said to the tortoise "I will not insult you
     again [*lit.* second time]." '

Text 2   **Doobbiičč-u**   **bank'o**   **aɗɗ-a**   **hasʔir-ino**   "A Lion Wanted to Marry a Thunder'

     doobbiičč-u   bank'o   aɗɗ-a   hasʔir-ino
     lion-NOM   thunder   marry-INF   want-3MS.PPERF
     'A Lion Wanted to Marry a Thunder'

1.   doobbiičč-u   seenne   aɗɗ-a[40]   hasʔir-e   bank'o-te
     lion-NOM   girls   take-INF   want-3MS.PERF   thunder-of

     ʔaydd-i-wa   mar-i-no
     family-EE-towards   go-3MS.PPERF
     'A lion wanted to marry a girl and went to the family of a thunder.'

2.   bank'o   hank'e   ʔane   gedee-te   y-ee   hede-e
     thunder   anger   me   like-COP.F   say-3MS.CONV   think-3MS.CONV
     'Thinking that thunder has the same degree of rage like him.'

---

[40] The expression **seenne aɗɗ-a** means 'to marry'. Its literal translation is 'taking girls'.

3. | bank'o-te | ʔama-no | "ballo | beetto-ʔya-we | | ʔamalaame-te; |
| thunder-of | mother-and | please | daughter-my-EMPH | | bad-tempered-COP.F |

| hank'o-se | di-dand-aato-we" | | y-i-tino |
| anger-her | NEG-able-2MS.IMPERF-EMPH | | say-EE-3FS.PPERF |

'And the mother of thunder said "please my daughter is a bad-tempered one. You will not withstand her rage." '

4. | hatto | y-ii-tee-nna | | "hank'o | ʔane | geešš-i-h-u |
| like that | say-EE-3FS.CONV-and | | anger | me | extent-EE-REL-NOM |

| ʔay-i | heeʔr-e-nna | | hatto | y-ii-ta-ʔe |
| who-NOM | live-3MS CONV-and | | like that | say-EE-3FS.IMPERF-me |

| y-e | č'oye-se | haʔr-a | giw-inó |
| say-3MS.CONV | thing-her | go-INF | refuse-3MS.PPERF |

'When she said this he refused to accept the matter saying "why she says like this since there is no one who can be so enraged like me." '

5. | haaʔr-a | giw-í-ta | | maayye | y-i-te,[41] | | "hanni[42] |
| go-INF | refuse-3MS.PERF-when | | alright | say-EE-3FS.CONV | | EMPH |

| ʔanf-eemmo-na | ʔat-i-no | ʔise-no |
| know-1PL.IMPERF-PART | you-NOM-and | she-and |

| bareende-ʔne | ma geešši-te-ro | leell-i-š-še-ʔe" |
| courage-your | what so far-COP.F-if | be seen-EE-CAUS-3PL.IMPER-me |

| y-i-tino |
| say-EE-3FS.PPERF |

'When he refused to go she consented and said "we will see; both of you show me how much is your courage!" '

6. | ʔis-i-no | bareende-si | kule, | gat'igal-u | baal-u |
| he-NOM-and | courage-his | tell-3MS.CONV | wild animal-NOM | all-NOM |

| ʔass-e | ʔayrris-anno-si | gara | č'oyr-ino |
| do-3MS.CONV | respect-3MS.IMPERF | way | speak-3MS.PPERF |

---

[41] Sidaama is rich in idiomatic expressions involving compound verbs. In sentence (5) above **maayye y-** 'consent/agree' is composed of **maayye** 'alright/okay' and **y-** 'say'.

[42] Sidaama has several emphatic particles. One of this is **hanni** which is used to stress the imperative or jussive.

'And he spoke about his courage and talked about how all wild animals respect him.'

7. **tenne**[43] **leell-i-š-a-te**   **bado** **ʔise-ti** **dag-gú**
   then   be seen-EE-CAUS-INF-for turn   her-REL arrive-3FS.PERF
   'Then her turn reached to show this [courage].'

8. **hakkiinni** **mitto** **ʔafoo fuššidʼ-dʼe-nna**   **t'ot'-atto-nna**
   From there one   word take out-3FS.COP-and spark-NMZ-and

   belek'o **ʔikk-i-tino**
   lightening happen-EE-3FS.PPERF
   'And then when she uttered a single word a spark and a lightening took place.'

9. **hatte**   **yanna-ra** **doobb-i-čč-u**   **mas-e**   **fuutt-ino**
   that (F) time-at   lion-EE-SGV-NOM be scared-3MS.CONV fart-3MS.PPERF
   At that moment the lion was scared and farted.'

10. **hakko** **bank'o** **hank'o-nna**   **bareende** **ʔiso** **roore**
    there   thunder anger-and   courage   him   more

    ʔikk-i-tino-ta   **ʔaf-e,**   **ʔamale-no**
    be-EE-3FS.PPERF-REL know-3MS.CONV conduct-and

    dand-ee   **ʔaf-anno-kki-ta**   **ʔama-te**
    withstand-3MS.CONV know-3MS.IMPERF-NEG mother-to

    č'oyr-e,   **ʔagur-e,**   **ʔaydd-i-si-ra**   **haʔr-ino,**
    tell-3MS.CONV leave-3MS.CONV family-EE-his-to go-3MS.PPERF

    y-i-noonni
    say-EE- IMPRS.PPERF

    'It is said that then and there he understood that a thunder was greater than him regarding rage and courage. He told her mother that he can't withstand her [that of the thunder] conduct and left [everything] and went back to his family.'

---

[43] Note that the contrast between **ténne** 'then, now' and **tenné** 'this (f.) one' is that of stress.

Bibliography

Abebe Gebre-Tsadik. 1982. *Derived nominals in Sidamo*. Unpublished Senior essay, Addis Ababa University: Addis Ababa. (Unpublished Senior Essay)

Abebe Gebre-Tsadik, *et al*. 1985. "The Verb Morphophonemics of Five Highland East Cushitic Languages Including Burji", *Afrikanistische Arbeitspapiere 2*. Universitat zu Koln.

Ameka, Felix. 1992. Interjections. the Universal yet Neglected Part of Speech. *Journal of Pragmatics*. 18. pp. 101-118.

Ameka, Felix. 1994. Interjections. In. Asher, R.E. and J.M.Y. Simpson (eds.), *The Encyclopedia of Language and Linguistics*, vol. 4, pp. 1712-1715. Oxford: Pergamon. Press.

Anbessa Teferra. 1984. *Sidamo Verb Morphology. Some Inflections and Derivations*. Addis Ababa University. (Unpublished B.A. Thesis.)

Anbessa Teferra. 1987. *Complement Clauses in Sidamo*. Addis Ababa University, Faculty of Graduate Studies. (Unpublished M.A. thesis)

Anbessa Teferra. 1987b. "Ballissha. Women's Speech among the Sidama", *Journal of Ethiopian Studies*, Vol. 20, pp. 44-59. Addis Ababa University.

Anbessa Teferra. 2000. *A Grammar of Sidaama*. Jerusalem. Hebrew University. (Unpublished Ph.D. dissertation,)

Anbessa Teferra. 2002. "Palatalization in Sidaama", *Proceedings of the XIVth International Conference of Ethiopian Studies* (Addis Ababa, 2000), Baye Yimam et al, eds., pp. 1674-1678. Addis Ababa: Institute of Ethiopian Studies.

Anbessa Teferra. 2007. "The structure of Sidaama nouns", *From beyond the Mediterranean* (Akten des 7 internationalen Semitohemitistenknogresses, Berlin 2004), Rainer Voigt, ed., pp. 185-195. Berlin: Shaker.

Anbessa Teferra. 2012. *A grammar of Sidaama. phonology, morphology, and syntax*. Saarbrücken: LAP Lambert. 200 pp.

Baye Yimam. 1986. *The Phrase Structures of Ethiopian Oromo*. (Unpublished Ph. D. Dissertation). University of London: School of Oriental and African Studies.

Bender, M. L. 1974. "Mutual intelligibility within Sidamo". *Congrès International de Linguistiqu Sémitique et Chamito-Sémitique* (Paris 1969), A. Caquot and D. Cohen, eds., pp. 159-169. The Hague: Mouton.

106

Bender, M. L. and R. L. Cooper 1974. . "Mutual intelligibility within Sidamo",*Lingua 27*: pp. 32-52.

Bender, et al. 1976. *Language in Ethiopia.* London: Oxford University Press.

Bender, M.L., ed. 1976. *The Non-Semitic Languages of Ethiopia.* East Lansing: African Studies Center, Michigan State University.

Bender, M. L., J. Donald Bowen, Robert L. Cooper, and Charles A. Ferguson, eds. 1976. *Language in Ethiopia.* London: Oxford University Press.

British and Foreign Bible Society. 1933. *St. Mark's Gospel in Sidamo.* London.

Bruno, Macani. 1990. *A Small Grammar of the Sidamo Language.* Miqe: Catholic Mission. (Unpublished Mimeograph).

Central Statistical Authority. 2010. *The 2007 Population and Housing Census of Ethiopia.* Statistical Report for for Southern Nations, Nationalities and Peoples' Region, Addis Ababa.

Cerulli, Enrico. 1938. *La lingua e la storia dei Sidamo* (Studi Etiopici II.) Roma: Istituto per l'Oriente.

Comrie, B. 1981. *Language Universals and Linguistic Typology.* Oxford: Blackwell Publishers.

Crystal, David. 1991. *A Dictionary of Linguistics and Phonetics.* Blackwell Publishers.

Indrias et. Al. et.al. 2007. *Sidaama-Amaarunna-Inglizete Qalla Borraasincho* (Sidaama-Amharic-English Dictionary). Addis Ababa: Master Printing Press.

Dingemanse, Mark. 2011a. *The Meaning and Use of Ideophones in Siwu.* Ph.D Dissertation, Nijmegen. Radboud University.

Dixon, R.M.W. 1982. *Where Have All the Adjectives Gone? and oOher Essays in Semantics and Syntax.* Berlin/ New York/Amsterdam: Mouton.

Ethiopian Bible Society. *Haaro Gondooro.* (Sidaama New Testament).

Gasparini, Armido. 1977. *A Collection of Various Sentences, Idioms, Exercises and Proverbs in Sidamo Language.* Awasa: Catholic Church. (mimeograph)

Gasparini Armido. 1978. *Grammatica Practica della Lingua Sidamo.* Awasa. (mimeograph)

Gasparini Armido. 1983. *Sidamo-English Dictionary.* Bologna: Editrice Missionara Italiana.

Girum Tesfaye. 2013. *Ideophones in Sidaama: Documentation and Description.* Addis Ababa: Addis Ababa University. (Unpublished M.A. Thesis)

Gragg, G. 1976. Oromo of Wallegga. In M. Bender (ed.), *The Non-Semitic Languages of Ethiopia.* East Lansing, MSU.

Greenberg, J. H. (ed), 1963. *Universals of Language.* Cambridge, Mass: MIT Press.

Hayward, R.J. 1975. `Middle Voice Verb Forms in Eastern Cushitic', *Transactions of the Philological Society*, pp. 203-24.

Hudson, Grover. 1969. "Towards a Generative Phonology of Sidamo," paper presented to *Language Study Group of Ethiopia*, Addis Ababa. mimeogr, 14pp.

Hudson, Grover. 1976a. "Highland East Cushitic", in *The Non-Semitic Languages of Ethiopia*. East Lansing: African Studies Center, Michigan State University.

Hudson, Grover. 1981. "The Highland East Cushitic family vine". *Sprache und Geschichte in Afrika* 3. pp. 97-124.

Hudson, Grover. 1983. *Highland East Cushitic Dictionary.* Hamburg: Buske.

Hudson, Grover. 2005. "Highland East Cushitic languages", *Encyclopedia of Language and Linguistics*, 2nd ed., Keith Brown, ed., pp. 294-298. Elsevier: Oxford.

Hudson, Grover. 2007a. "Highland East Cushitic morphology", *Morphologies of Asian and African Languages*, vol. 1, Alan M. Kaye, ed., pp. 529-545. Winona Lake, IN: Eisenbrauns.

Kawachi, Kazuhiro. 2007. *A Grammar of Sidaama (Sidamo), a Cushitic Language of Ethiopia.* Ph.D. Dissertation. Buffalo, NY: University at Buffalo.

Kawachi, Kazuhiro. 2008. "Middle voice and reflexive in Sidaama", *Proceedings of the the 40th Annual Meeting of the Chicago Linguistic Society* (2004), vol. 2, N. Adams et al eds., pp. 119-134. Chicago: Chicago Linguistic Society.

Leslau, Wolf. 1952a. "The influence of Sidamo on the Ethiopic languages of Gurage. *Language* 28. pp. 63-81.

Leslau, Wolf. 1959. "Sidamo features in South Ethiopic phonology". *Journal of the American Oriental Society* 79. pp. 1-7.

Leslau, Wolf. 1980. "Proto-*Sidamo *z*". *Afrika und Übersee* 63. pp. 119-129.

Lonfernini, Bruno. 1971. *I Sidamo, un Antico Popolo Cuscita.* Bologna: Editrice Nigrizia.

Moreno, Martino Mario. 1940. *Manuale di Sidamo,* Milano: Mondadori.

Moseley C. and Asher R.E. 1994. *Atlas of the World's Languages.* London: Routledge.

Owens, Jonathan. 1985. *A Grammar of Harar Oromo.* Hamburg: Buske.

Palmer, F.R. 1970. "Cushitic," *Current Trends in Linguistics* VI, ed. Th.K. Sebeok, The Hague, pp. 571-85.

Proclamation No. 1/1995 (*Federal Negarit Gazeta,* August 21, 1995, Addis Ababa).

Radford, Andrew. 1981. *Transformational Syntax.* Cambridge University Press.

Radford, Andrew. 1988. *Transformational Grammar.* Cambridge University Press.

Schneider-Blum, Gertrud 2007a. *A Grammar of Alaaba. A Higland East Cushitic Language of Ethiopia.* (Cushitic Language Studies, 25.) Cologne: Köppe.

Senayait Lemma. 1982. *Morphophonemics of Sidamo.* Unpublished Senior essay, Addis Ababa University: Addis Ababa.

Shimelis Gizaw. 1998. *Sidaamu Afii Maammashsha* [Proverbs of the Sidaama Language]. Addis Ababa: Ethiopian Languages Research Center. 144 pp.

Shack, W.A. 1966. *The Gurage. A People of the ensete Culture.* International African Institute: London.

Sim, Ronald. 1989. *Predicate Conjoining in Hadiyya. A Head-Driven PS Grammar.* (Unpublished Ph. D. Thesis.) University of Edinburgh: Department of Linguistics.

Tolo, Arne. 1998. *Sidaama and Ethiopian. The Emergence of Mekane Yesus Church in Sidama.* Uppsala (Studia Missionaria Upsaliensia LXIX).

Treis, Yvonne. 2008. *A Grammar of Kambaata (Part 1): Phonology, Nominal Morphology, and Non-Verbal Predication.* (Cushitic Language Studies, 26.) Cologne: Köppe.

Tucker, A. N. and Margaret A. Bryan. 1966. *Linguistic Analyses. the Non-Bantu Languages of North-Eastern Africa* (Handbook of African Languages). International African Institute: Oxford University Press.

Wedekind, Klaus. 1980. "Sidamo, Darasa (Gedeo), Burji. phonological differences and likenesses". *Journal of Ethiopian Studies* 14 [1976-79]. pp. 131-176.

Wedekind, Klaus. 1990. *Generating narratives. interrelationships of knowledge, text variants, and Cushitic focus strategies.* Berlin: Mouton de Gruyter.

Yri, Kjell Magne. 2004. "Orthography and phonology in Sidaama afoo (Sidamo)". *Journal of Ethiopian Studies* 37.1 pp. 41-56.

Yri, Kjell Magne. 2007. "Nouns and adjectives in Sidaamu Afó", *Omotic and Cushitic Studies Papers from the Fourth Cushitic Omotic Conference* (Leiden, 10-12 April 2003), Azeb Amha, Maarten Mous, Graziano Savà, eds., pp. 261-268. Cologne: Koeppe.

Yri, Kjell Magne. 2011. "The singulative in Sidaaamu Afó". *Folia Orientalia* 47, part II. pp. 117-136.

Languages of the World/Materials

LINCOM´s Descriptive Grammar Series